American Kestrels in Modern Falconry

Third Expanded Edition

By Matthew Mullenix

Western Sporting
Sheridan, Wyoming, USA

Frontispiece by
American Kestrel by Steven Hein

Third Revised Edition © 2002 Matthew R. Mullenix
Baton Rouge, Louisiana

Original Copyright © 1997
First Edition 1996
Second Edition 1997
Third Printing 1997
Fourth Printing 1998
Third Edition 2002
Sixth Printing 2007
Seventh Printing 2019

Published by
Western Sporting
730 Crook Street
Sheridan, Wyoming USA
www.westernsporting.com

Printed in the United States of America

ISBN 978-1-888357-05-9

ACKNOWLEDGMENTS

The inspiration for this book comes from many sources. I was introduced to kestrels by Jennifer and Tom Coulson of Pearl River, Louisiana, master falconers who shared freely of their experience and hospitality. I am grateful also to Ricky Schomburg, who was my sponsor and showed me how to catch quarry. That falconry could be a sport of exacting detail and style was proven to me by Joel Volpi, Eric Edwards, Jim Ince and Brian Millsap. For the basic format of this book, I am indebted to Harry McElroy, who set the standard for a hard-working falconry reference. Loftier goals were found in the elegance of Jack Mavrogordato's *A Hawk for the Bush,* and the sheer endurance of E.B. Michell's *The Art and Practice of Hawking*: two books every falconer should own.

Special thanks go to my proofreaders (many of whom are named above), and also to Bruce Haak for a fine review of this book; to Bill Oakes for taking a chance on an earlier version of my manuscript and to David Frank for creating the beautiful book now in your hands. But I am especially grateful to my wife Shelly, who knows her husband well and married him anyway.

Matthew Mullenix
Baton Rouge, Louisiana, USA

To Phoebe, somewhere in central Florida.

Matthew Mullenix & Phoebe (S.E. Female American Kestrel).

ABOUT THE ARTIST

Steve Hein is one of the fortunate few who pursues his lifelong passion for wildlife and calls it work. After earning a degree in business, he immediately embarked on a career as a wildlife artist. Self taught, Steve quickly gained national recognition through his work with conservation groups like Ducks Unlimited, Quail Unlimited and The National Wild Turkey Federation. He has received numerous awards for his work and garnered Georgia Power Company, Nations Bank and Coca-Cola as corporate clients.

As a free-lance artist, Steve was keenly interested in birds of prey and lured to the art of falconry. Over the past 15 years he has had the opportunity to train and fly several species including, with considerable insight from the author, the American kestrel. In 1991, Steve was given the rare opportunity to combine his talents to develop the Center for Wildlife Education and The Lamar Q. Ball, Jr. Raptor Center at Georgia Southern University. Serving as the director, Steve shares his fascination for raptors and wildlife with young and old alike.

Steve lives in Statesboro, Georgia with his wife Kathy, son Adam, daughter Meredith and twin girls Mallory and Colleen. Despite an often hectic schedule, during the fall and winter he is often riding the back roads in pursuit of the perfect duck slip.

Artist, Grace and labrador "Sam".

ABOUT THE COVER

"Downsized"

by Steve Hein

The cover painting depicts North America's smallest longwing, a male kestrel closing on an English house sparrow. The scene portrayed is a reflection of the artist's past falconry experiences of hunting with this diminutive, but capable kestrel. *"The small contribution of artwork and the chance to work with the author, an accomplished falconer and dear friend, is deeply appreciated."*

CONTENTS

Illustration & Photographic Credits

Front Cover	*Steve Hein* (Gouache on board)	" Downsized"
Frontispiece	*Steve Hein* (Pencil on paper)	"Nice Flight!"
Page 9	*Unknown* (Photograph)	*Matthew Mullenix & Pheobe*
Page 11	*Frank Fortune* (Photograph)	*Steve Hein, Grace & labrador "Sam"*
Page 20	*Steve Hein* (Pencil on paper)	*Kestrel in Flight*
Page 24	*Steve Hein* (Pencil on paper)	*Eyas Kestrel in Nest*
Page 26	*Bruce Haak* (Photograph)	*Kestrel on eggs*
Page 28	*Archives of American Falconry* (Photograph)	"Bobby"
Page 32	*Jim Wilson* (Photograph)	"Nova" on starling
Page 34	*Unknown* (Photograph)	"Tycho" & "Ella"
Page 37	*Tom Smylie* (Photograph)	*Adult male kestrel*
Page 38	*Bruce Haak* (Photograph)	*Kestrel in net*
Page 41	*David Frank* (Photograph)	*Tail feathers*
Page 43	*Tom Smylie* (Photograph)	*Kestrel on bal-chatri*
Page 44	*Steve Hein* (Pencil on paper)	*Kestrel Reaching for Tidbit*
Page 50	*Steve Hein* (Pencil on paper)	*Vignette of equipment*
Page 53	*David Frank* (Photograph)	*Tethering system*

FOREWORD

The first edition of Matt Mullenix's book, *American Kestrels In Modern Falconry*, made it clear to me that the art of training and hawking with kestrels had passed me by. Like so many falconers before me, I was initiated into the care and training of raptors with a kestrel, but never encouraged to take them seriously. Back in the 1960s, a kestrel was a stepping stone to a red-tailed hawk, nothing more. Today, North America's most ubiquitous raptor has also become one of the most useful in the service of falconers.

My first experience with a kestrel came nearly four decades ago. Ignorant but enthusiastic, I attempted falconry with most of the trappings a preteen could purchase or fabricate. My readings had helped fuel the fire of fascination with falconry, but could provide no practical experience. In the end, what I needed most was the guidance of a mentor. When training a kestrel, one needs a specialized mentor indeed.

One summer when I was in high school I had two kestrels, a recently fledged male and a female that were salvaged from a pet store in southern California. Their primaries had been cut short and required a full imping job on both wings to restore their powers of flight. Coincidentally, one of my friends had a quail pen that was regularly frequented by house sparrows, so we were able to acquire numerous "volunteers" to teach these kestrels to hunt. In time, it became clear that the female preferred the direct line of attack. She simply left the fist, chased her quarry out of the air and captured it in cover. The male, however, seemed inclined to wait-on. He regularly flew about 100 feet overhead, looking for quarry to appear. Flying on a beach gave this kestrel the opportunity to use the wind, and the well-timed release of sparrows encouraged him to fly in true game-hawking style. In time, he would pursue wild sparrows in this manner. I left for college in late summer, which ended this experiment. But my impression was that this particular kestrel had become quite comfortable with this tactic.

Because the kestrel has been down-played in the literature as both a beginner's bird and one incapable of actually catching wild quarry, there was no incentive for many budding falconers to apply themselves with kestrels. Now, Matt Mullenix brings a unique philosophy to hawking with kestrels and conveys the parameters of this discipline in clear prose. After reading Matt's book, I understand how the directed, concerted effort he advocates pays off in hunting success on wild quarry. In hindsight, it seems odd that the hunting prowess of the continent's most common raptor should be so overlooked. However, the management of this species, underpinned by diligent attention to weight, diet and equipment, is the time-consuming and all-important key to success with it. Few other raptors are out of sorts when a mere two grams overweight. An added concern is that the diminutive size of the kestrel leaves it constantly exposed to the potential dangers of predators and pirates when it is pursuing or subduing quarry. Judging by Matt's experience with European kestrels, a much maligned species among falconers in western Europe, this management and training system may also offer an avenue for employing this cousin-species to greater good in its native land.

One important feature of this book is that Matt shows how the natural inclinations and hunting style of an American kestrel can be applied to hawking unprotected small birds in a wide range of rural and urban environments. He demonstrates that the short chase, especially one initiated from the window of an automobile, is the most effective way of taking quarry on open ground with a kestrel. While kestrels have the courage to capture birds larger than themselves, they lack the physical endurance for long, high-speed chases, so exemplary in the flight of merlins. However, the short-range convenience of kestrels, coupled with the fact that they can be flown in enclosed, highly urbanized environments, makes them a raptor of great utility.

To my way of thinking, the only thing trained kestrels fail to demonstrate is a dramatic hunting style in the form of a fast, vertical stoop. Anyone who has watched wild kestrels hunt, protect their nest sites, and badger other raptors can attest to their power and tenacity in the air. Surely the next phase in the evolution of falconry with kestrels will be the development of dependable waiting-on flights over pinned quarry. The introduction of kite and balloon training may cement the tendency of a reluctant flier to take a consistent pitch. Coupled with the proliferation of house sparrows and starlings over the rapidly urbanizing landscape of temperate North America, this would seem a proper fit of hawk and quarry. Even in reduced scale, the "go up, come down" aspects of a falcon's hunting flight are apt to generate devotees to this exciting form of small-game hawking.

Bruce Haak
Eagle, Idaho, USA

I INTRODUCTION

Standing in the buffet line on the night of the field meet banquet, I was able to overhear a conversation from a table behind me. Actually, as drinks had already been served, I was quite unable not to hear it. Two local falconers were discussing the day's hawking when one asked the other, "So what'd the kestrel catch?" The speaker's tone was even and the question sincere. I had come to expect some pretty strange dialogue from this group, but this question surprised me. I wandered in the table's direction to hear more.

Could it be that someone brought a trained kestrel to a Louisiana Hawking Club meet? These were dedicated hawkers, almost entirely given to group hunting with the relentless Harris' hawk. High local rabbit populations and grueling all day excursions meant few falconers went home empty handed. In this club, failure to catch quarry is a serious faux pas.

What could a kestrel possibly have caught? Imagine my surprise when the falconer replied, "Three starlings and a grackle. She could have taken more, but we had to meet the other guys for lunch."

I was hooked. Bird-catching kestrels were a new twist in my developing falconry paradigm. As I learned more that evening, I found that many of the club members had flown kestrels at birds with regular success. Even at that meet, there were several kestrels in use. As caravans of falconers wound their way from one rabbit field to another, the small kestrels would be slipped at flocks of blackbirds feeding near the roadside. This technique proved so successful that individual kestrels could easily account for as many starlings as a Harris' hawk could rabbits. This is how the diminutive, much derided kestrel earned the respect of such no-nonsense hawkers as these.

So this is where I will begin: American kestrels are capable of regularly catching house sparrows, starlings and occasionally larger birds. Kestrels are more than a match for these quarries and have been flown successfully at such for decades. Further, successful trained kestrels are not exceptional individuals of an otherwise unsuitable species—birds of all ages, origins, sizes and both sexes have proven equally capable.

What I write in the following pages is an overview of the hunting methods and captive management techniques by which hawking kestrels can be maintained. The ideas and opinions expressed are not entirely original; as I have said, flying kestrels at starlings long precedes my experience with the sport. In this respect, I hope that I have accurately attributed credit where it is due.

CONSIDERATIONS

Several topics related to this form of falconry should be addressed before the reader continues. First, consider your quarry. Trained kestrels will catch dove and quail on rare occasion, but the size, speed and habitat of these species put them outside serious contention. Unless your circumstances are extraordinary, choose another hawk for serious dove and quail hunting.

Introduction

The most practical birds to hunt with a kestrel are starlings and house sparrows. These are common, readily caught, and they form the staple of kestrel hawking everywhere. Happily, they are introduced species and receive no federal protection. Native blackbirds (e.g., grackles and cowbirds of the family *Icteridae*) are also excellent kestrel quarries and in many states are legal to kill as depredating or nuisance wildlife.

Second, roadside hawking may in some states be considered a violation of laws designed to prohibit shooting from a vehicle. That no firearms or game species are involved in "road-hawking" may seem a small point to a wildlife officer bent on writing a ticket. Many states do waive hunting restrictions for unprotected birds, but local traffic and wildlife sanctuary ordinances may still apply. If you practice this form of hunting, restrict yourself to private roads and property (e.g., industrial parks) and observe all local, state and federal laws.

Finally, if choosing the kestrel as your first falconry bird, marshal your resources. Discuss the subject with your sponsor, and take full advantage of the experience of others. Small raptors require precision weight control and equipment design. You will need a sharp eye, a light touch, the right tools and a talent for detail. What you find in the following chapters will help illustrate and develop the skills necessary for success. But the lion's share of the work is yours to do.

To every falconer game for a challenge, let me introduce a very worthy hunting partner: The American Kestrel.

A BRIEF NATURAL HISTORY
WITH NOTES ON DIET
AND HUNTING

The American kestrel *(Falco sparverius)* is our smallest native longwing and the only breeding species of kestrel in the continental U.S. Individuals vary in size within every population, though northern birds tend to be larger than their southern counterparts (James, 1970). Small males may be as light as 70 grams and large females may exceed 165 grams.

Kestrel plumage also varies in color and pattern. Generally females are reddish-brown with dark barring and males a striking combination of red, blue, orange, black and white.

American kestrels are common throughout the U.S., though have declined in the Southeast possibly due to habitat loss (Stys, 1993). Kestrels are cavity nesters and often choose nest sites near open fields where insects, mice and field sparrows are plentiful (Hoffman and Collopy, 1987). Diet varies widely by region and season; some populations feed heavily on insects and lizards (Smallwood, 1987) and others largely on starlings, sparrows and rodents (Smith and Murphy, 1973). This difference may cause some to fear that their local kestrels are not up to the challenge of hawking birds. I would counter that my most productive kestrel (Phoebe) hailed from the center of Dr. Smallwood's study area in Florida, and she caught birds with great success.

American Kestrels in Modern Falconry

Many consider the American kestrel to be primarily insectivorous. In fact, numerous studies have proven our kestrel dines predominantly on vertebrate quarry (i.e., mammals, birds and reptiles). A good example of a bird truly dependent on invertebrate prey is the mockingbird *(Mimus polyglottis)*. Kestrels have been known to eat mockingbirds but never the reverse.

Of course, wild kestrels do prey on insects. If one counts the number of items eaten on a given day, insects may even prove most numerous, especially in the warmer months. But for the same reason that ten nickels are still less than one dollar, ten insects do not equal one starling. What makes the difference is "biomass," the measurement of an animal's diet that includes the weight of each item consumed.

Wild kestrel on eggs in nest box.

A Brief Natural History

Johnsgard (1990) provides an excellent illustration of this in a chapter devoted to the kestrel's natural history. It reads in part:

> *Smith and Murphy (1973) estimate the kestrel's diet in Utah to consist of 38 percent mammals (compared to 26 percent numerically), 57 percent birds (compared to 16 percent numerically), and 2 percent invertebrates (compared to 52 percent numerically). The most important vertebrate prey were starlings (Sturnus vulgaris) and deer mice (Peromyscus maniculatus), these two species contributing over 60 percent of the total biomass intake.*

Another popular notion attributed to the kestrel, but not supported by research, is that it hunts chiefly by hovering. In fact, our kestrels rarely hover (Balgooyen, 1976) and are more likely to seek, attack and capture prey from a perched position. This is significant from the falconer's perspective as the American kestrel is a more effective still-hunter than aerial predator. This helps explain why most of a trained kestrel's quarry will be taken by surprise and with a short direct slip.

"Bobby" American kestrel circa 1933
Courtesy: Archives of American Falconry.

III   *USE IN FALCONRY*

Kestrels have a long history in falconry. In medieval Europe, the Common kestrel *(Falco tinnunculus)* was reserved for the novice falconer. It was poorly regarded and little used for actual hunting. The traditionally low esteem afforded this species persists to the present day, particularly among British authors (Ford, 1992), and may have tainted the reputation of our native kestrel.

In light of the demonstrable success of the American kestrel, the negative view of the European bird may change. It is roughly twice the weight of our kestrel and takes a variety of avian prey in the wild, from sparrows to wood pigeons (Village, 1990). A few European and African falconers have succeeded with the Common kestrel, and my own brief experience with the bird convinced me of its potential: I flew a captive bred eyas of unknown sex (flying weight 170 grams) with success at a wide range of species. In three months, this kestrel took 48 birds: including sparrows, starlings, mourning doves, pigeons, a snipe and a boat-tailed grackle (Mullenix, 1997). Most birds were taken on the ground with a close slip, or in the case of the pigeons, at night with the aid of a flashlight. However, this kestrel was extremely aerial, waiting-on naturally and at length, so perhaps that style of hunting would be better suited to the bird than the method I chose.

American Kestrels in Modern Falconry

Early accounts of trained American kestrels listed modest successes; Frank and John Craighead chased small birds with kestrels as boys, and a young Fran Hamerstrom flew her kestrel at sparrows roosting in the ivy covered wall of her childhood home. One early reference to a serious attempt with the kestrel comes from James N. Layne, writing in the April, 1943 issue of the <u>Journal of the Falconer's Association of America</u>. Layne's eyas female caught nineteen sparrows and a robin in his urban Chicago neighborhood before being killed by a man with a BB-gun. Anyone familiar with urban sparrow hawking will find Layne's account plausible and familiar. He writes:

> *I threw her off again and she dashed over to the construction and shot behind a light in the ceiling. A moment later she parachuted down to the sidewalk almost at the feet of a passerby, with a sparrow in her talons...I do not feel that any other type of hawk would hunt and perform as well under similar conditions.*

Today Layne's comments have largely proven true. American kestrels are uniquely suited to hawking developed areas, with starlings and house sparrows as its chief quarries.

With the aid of a close slip, kestrels can take hundreds of starlings in a season. English sparrows are as readily caught and their pursuit can take a surprising variety of forms. Flights at these species are generally short; whether successful or not, few will extend beyond view. This makes the kestrel an ideal choice for hawking the enclosed suburban landscape in which most of us live.

Kestrels' speed over extended distance is not great, but they are aggressive, nimble and determined in close quarters. Both wild and trained, they are successful predators of quarry ranging from a few grams to twice their own weight. Kestrels prefer spotting quarry from a perch, but they will adopt the more active hunting styles of merlins and accipiters when appropriate. They will ambush birds with a long, low profile approach or run them down in cover after a brief sprint. They can and will catch sparrows on the wing in a vertical stoop.

In my view, American kestrels are like tiny prairie falcons *(Falco mexicanus)*. Both have tough, pliable feathers, relatively long tails, large heads and stout toes. Both species regularly take mammalian in addition to avian prey and both are willing to attack large quarry in relation to their body size, often binding to them on the ground. And though exacting weight control improves performance in most trained raptors; prairie falcons and kestrels both require particular attention in this area. The range of weights at which they will respond well is narrow when compared to peregrines and merlins—particularly when speaking of passage birds (see Ken Tuttle and Jennifer Coulson in their respective chapters of McElroy's Desert Hawking...with a Little Help from My Friends, 1996).

Passage female "Nova" on starling.

(Note to reader: Please refer to chart on page 124 for particulars of the kestrels depicted in this book.)

$\mathbb{IV}$ _CHOICE OF A BIRD_

One's choice of any hawk may include eyas or passage, male or female. Each offers different rewards and challenges. Current regulations allow for haggard kestrels to be taken, so an additional choice may deserve consideration.

Eyas, Passage or Haggard?

Haggard and eyas kestrels are uniquely challenging. Many adult kestrels remain nervous and difficult to manage in captivity. Conversely, most eyases are extremely tame but are prone to constant screaming (food begging) at home and in the field. Curiously, both eyases and haggards can develop into incorrigible carriers.

Jennifer Coulson (1996) states a preference for the eyas, and her great success with eyas kestrels gives her opinion weight. In her experience, the eyas is more easily conditioned to a variety of flight styles, particularly to bolting off the fist at flushed sparrows. However, having seen Jennifer repeatedly catch sparrows off the fist with both eyas and passage kestrels, I am tempted to credit her success to hard work and skill, rather than to any advantage offered by the eyas.

I have flown two haggard kestrels, both females, that differed like night and day. One was a large northern migrant that flew best at 125 grams; the other a small southeastern resident bird with a flying weight of 85 grams. The first kestrel remained wild throughout her short career and carried (or attempted to) nearly every kill she made. The other kestrel began tame, remained so until her release, and carried not one of the numerous small birds she caught over three seasons. Of these two kestrels, the first is probably the more typical haggard in behavior.

One trait these two hawks did share was speed. In my estimation, each was capable of speed approaching a merlin's, though for not so long a duration. Both could take birds in flight, sometimes intercepting prey already on the wing when the chase began. Whether speed is a trait typical of haggard kestrels, I cannot say.

"Tycho" (adult passage male) & "Ella" (passage female)
perched together for comparison.
(Otherwise not a recommended perching arrangement.)

Choice of Bird

My preference is for the passage bird. They grow nearly as tame with careful management as an eyas, and they have the potential to match the speed and style of the haggard if flown regularly. Taking passage kestrels for falconry does not detract from the breeding stock, as does the taking of haggards and unlike the eyas, passagers may be released at any time.

It is a persistent myth that passage kestrels are "wed" to invertebrate prey. This simply isn't so. With consistent, quality slips, passage kestrels quickly take to hunting birds. Conversely, all trained kestrels will catch bugs if the opportunity presents itself. If for no other reasons, one should prefer a kestrel unlikely to scream, yet tame enough to manage easily—this is the passager.

Whichever age of hawk you choose to take, hard work in producing good slips is the greatest predictor of success. In the hands of hard-working falconers, I have seen eyas, passage and haggard kestrels all develop into deadly bird hawks.

Male or female?

There is no bird a male can catch that a female can't, but there are several quarries a female will find easier to subdue. On this basis, the female seems the obvious choice. However, males and females are equally capable on sparrows and starlings; as these are the most common quarries, both sexes deserve consideration.

Male and female kestrels differ more greatly in build than their relative weight would suggest. On close comparison, one finds the female proportionately more robust. She has larger feet, a deeper beak, a wider stance and broader shoulders. She has less trouble with large quarry and is a more efficient killer across the board. When one compares a small southeastern male to a large northern female, the difference can be striking—she can be twice his size.

But greater size is not always a plus. Large females may dispatch and carry quarry more easily than males. For example, a large female of mine would kill starlings almost at impact and could carry one twenty yards in a flash. My males, by contrast, typically had to bring sparrows to the ground to control them and were not able to carry larger birds more than a few feet.

As a general guide, the sex of kestrel you choose may depend on the quarry most readily available to you. Three popular quarries, English sparrows, starlings and common grackles (legal quarry when depredating), average 28 grams, 80 grams and 114 grams respectively (Dunning, 1993). A falconer happy to hunt sparrows and starlings will find the male kestrel perfectly suitable; those wishing to add grackles to the larder will appreciate the slightly greater weight and strength of the female. Any attempt to catch the imposing (214 gram) boat-tailed grackle will require a large female (or two), and here perhaps the natural boldness of the eyas will lend some advantage.

Adult male kestrel.

Removing a kestrel from a net.

V *TRAPPING THE PASSAGER*

The most exciting kestrel trapping I have enjoyed was during the fall migration on the Gulf Coast of Florida. We used a lure sparrow and a trio of small dho-ghazza nets arranged in the sand. The nets were strung to poles on sliding brass rings and set to drop at the slightest contact. In the wake of a cold front, and with a little luck, kestrels and other raptors would pass our trapping blind in good numbers. As the birds appeared at a distance, the fluttering sparrow would prompt fast, contour-hugging attacks ending with the welcome "clink-clink" sound of the collapsing nets.

Beach trapping, for all its excitement, can be an elaborate affair and inconvenient for those living far from the coast. Fortunately, passage kestrels can be secured much more easily with a bal-chatri. The "bc" is essentially a small cage adorned with monofilament nooses designed to tangle around the toes of a raptor. A bait animal is placed inside the cage, and the trap is set (under constant supervision) where the raptor is likely to see it. It is an ancient and effective method for safely trapping birds of prey.

In my experience, English sparrows are better bait than are pet store mice. Mice are prone to sitting tight in one corner of the trap and have been known to make a nest of your carefully tied nooses. Some kestrels find large mice intimidating and multiple mice may possibly deter them. I have never seen one refuse a frantic house sparrow.

The trap's nooses should be approximately an inch in diameter and evenly spaced, though not necessarily in great numbers. If the bait is active, the kestrel will typically run across the trap until captured. According to raptor biologist Brian Millsap, a low ceiling on the bal-chatri (1.5–2.0 inches) is most effective for keeping kestrels interested in the bait animal. The trap itself need not be more than 12–14 inches on a side.

With roadside trapping, a few words of warning are in order. Falconers' use of Interstate rights of way have more than once aroused the suspicions of the Highway Patrol. Driving under the minimum speed limit, stopping without warning and use of the median as a turning lane have all been considered just cause for investigation. Recently in the State of Georgia, a falconer was cited for "trapping fur-bearing animals within 100 yards of a public roadway."

It may be safer and more productive to avoid the Interstate altogether. In the southeastern United States, two lane rural routes rolling through agricultural or pastoral landscapes are prime habitat for wintering kestrels, particularly the females, which prefer open fields to the more wooded areas frequented by males (Smallwood, 1987).

Having spotted a likely candidate, lay the baited bal-chatri on the exposed shoulder or the road as far as possible from passing cars. Don't be surprised if the kestrel flushes from this slight disturbance. Kestrels are sometimes easily spooked, though will rarely fly further than the next section of powerline. They may even flush back over the trap as you pass under them. In any event, one need not wait long for a response; kestrels always seem to be hungry, in spite of the fact that most are fat when trapped.

Immature Female   Mature Female   Male of any age*
(Feathers shown life size.)

*(*Generally there is no difference between immature
or mature male tail feathers.)*

Once the bird is snared, waste no time in reaching her. I have on several occasions raced against incoming raptors intent on an easy meal. A lengthy stay on the trap may also damage the kestrel's small toes and long tails. Extract the bird bare-handed, or with only a light glove. It is important to know the amount of pressure you exert on such small, delicate bodies. Of course, when bare handed, be aware that kestrels' first defense is a very potent bite!

It is not always possible to determine the age of a trapped kestrel, especially one taken late in the year. However, here are a few guidelines to follow: if a male exhibits a uniform cream or peach-colored breast with small, round spots down each side, he is probably an adult; juvenile males tend to have lighter colored but more heavily marked breast feathers than adults; if a female sports a wide black band at the distal end of her tail (twice as wide, or wider, than those above it) she is probably an adult; females in juvenile plumage tend to have uniformly narrow tail bands down to the tip.

Though kestrels undergo a partial first-year molt, those growing several new primaries in the fall are probably mature. Adult birds often show a pronounced orange color on their cere and feet, compared to the pale yellow of juvenile birds. Finally, if you find yourself unable to determine its age, simply toss the bird up and trap another a few hundred yards down the line. All else equal, the haggard birds should be released.

Once the kestrel is in hand, I generally place it in a dark cardboard box for the journey home. A folded towel on the bottom of the box gives the kestrel a surface firm enough to stand on, yet soft enough to prevent feather damage. Some falconers prefer to restrain the kestrel gently in a section of nylon stocking. This stocking is cut to fit so that its head is exposed above the shoulders and legs exposed below the tarsi. Thin strips of masking or electrical tape hold the stocking in place at these points, and the kestrel is hooded. If this method is used, be sure to prevent the kestrel's overheating and to remove it from the stocking promptly at home. Other falconers prefer to jess the kestrel in the car or trapping blind and allow it to travel hooded on a small perch or the gloved fist. However you transport your new kestrel home, weigh the bird shortly after you arrive. If socked or hooded, the kestrel can be placed easily on a gram scale and an initial weight recorded.

Kestrel trapped on a bal-chatri.

VI MANNING AND TRAINING

A trained kestrel, in addition to becoming a serious hunting partner, can soon become a member of the family. These small, attractive hawks quickly charm spouses and children, a fact not only benefiting the falconer but advantageous to the kestrel as well. To facilitate a kestrel's taming and training, I prefer to reserve a place for it in the family room, at least during the first few weeks of captivity. A three-foot by four-foot length of foam padding, covered by an equal measure of indoor/outdoor carpeting, makes a suitable location for the bow perch.

The kestrel's perch should be placed in view of family activities, indeed right in the mix of them. Exposure to people and pets should be initiated early. While this can be a stressful time for a new hawk, that's all the more reason to get through it promptly. The faster a kestrel grows tame in captivity, the healthier it will be.

The first moments of manning are the worst for falconer and kestrel alike. The kestrel may bate, bite, hang, scream or simply lie limp across the fist as if paralyzed. Some that seem unusually tame at first may simply be saving their tantrum for the next day. The advice and support of one's sponsor, and one's own past experience will help put this period in perspective. It is hard to imagine that in seven or ten days, the same kestrel will be flying across a room to take a tidbit from your glove.

Attempt the first feeding late on the evening of capture unless the kestrel is especially thin, in which case feed earlier. A fat kestrel may refuse the first feeding, but may take food readily the following morning. For a truly reticent kestrel, unwilling to eat on the second day, it is important to make repeated attempts at regular intervals until it concedes. Kestrels may be stubborn, but they will not let themselves starve.

A fresh sparrow or mouse will be familiar to the new kestrel and makes a good first meal. Once the kestrel is eating well, thawed sections of starling are handy as filler and tirings. I'll mention here and elsewhere the importance of maintaining kestrels on a diet of small, whole animals.

Water is often overlooked in a raptor's diet and is essential to a small hawk under stress. A few drops of water from a syringe or the fingertips will slow dehydration and will also help gain the kestrel's trust. Offering tidbits of food and water from one's fingers is a time-honored technique for manning hawks of all kinds, and it works equally well with kestrels.

Weight reduction is a necessary component of manning and training any wild raptor. It is also among falconry's greatest challenges. The rate of weight loss must be managed exactly in a small hawk; careless inaccuracy can have serious consequences. The Appendices list examples of kestrel flight weights and schedules of weight reduction, but these are not offered as absolutes. There is no substitute for simple vigilance when dropping a kestrel's weight.

For a healthy kestrel, weight reduction may proceed at two to three gram increments per day for the first week; during this time, the falconer should encourage short flights to the fist and continue exposure to family, friends and animals.

After the first week, weight loss must be slowed to one gram or less per day. Once the kestrel is flying outdoors, further reductions must be made in tenths of a gram.

Reducing a new hawk's weight and maintaining the weight of a trained one are closely related skills. A following section (Chapter X) will outline a simple method to both predict and control a kestrel's weight twenty-four hours in advance. This is essential to successful training and hunting, and its application to controlled weight reduction is obvious. When you reach that section, read it with both applications in mind.

Kestrels are often regarded as being docile and taming quickly. Falconers' fond memories of hand-raised kestrels may perpetuate this notion. While it may be true of eyases, my experience with passage and haggard birds has been very different. Should you happen to trap a sweet passage kestrel, one that pops back on the fist the first time and never bates or bites, God has truly blessed you.

In fact, some passage kestrels will remain aloof until they are fully trained and hunting. Keeping the kestrel hooded or isolated during the first two weeks will likely frustrate your efforts to tame her. Occasionally a falconer will attempt to delay weight reduction and training until their kestrel is completely tame. This is usually a mistake. Few kestrels will become tame without some reduction in weight and some progress made towards training. Once trained, a slightly balky kestrel is generally safe enough to fly at starlings, if not at more portable quarry like sparrows. By doing so, a kestrel often becomes tame with the establishment of a hunting routine and the repetition of returning to the falconer for food.

By the end of the fifth week of captivity, most passage kestrels will have finally calmed down. The ultimate tame kestrel will allow itself to be picked up around the body, happily accepting tidbits from one hand while being carried around in the other. This may seem excessive, but a small hawk that is to be picked up on small quarry and regularly examined for physical injury should be kept as tame as possible.

In training, kestrels do not differ significantly in schedule or technique from passage birds of other species (See Appendix 2 for one kestrel's training log). As with the red-tailed hawk, training stages are predictable and straightforward. Most lessons are simple and can be learned within the first few days:

1) Standing on the fist

2) Returning to the fist after a bate

3) Eating off the fist

4) Sitting on the perch

5) Returning to the perch after a bate

6) Hopping to the fist

7) Hopping to the lure

8) Flying on a creance outside*

9) Flying free outdoors

10) Catching quarry

The speed with which each step is completed seems to depend as much upon the kestrel as on the falconer. Some kestrels will hop to the fist the first night; others may take a week or more. Brian Millsap observes that kestrels (and other passage birds) may be slow at one stage but make up for it in the next. Given such variation in the completion of each stage, the process should take about four weeks between trapping and active hunting. However, I wouldn't be surprised to learn of someone hunting within two weeks, or conversely, to hear that a kestrel was still on the creance at five weeks. Just train as fast as your kestrel and common sense will allow.

At this stage, one peculiarity of the kestrel may become troublesome as some kestrels are extremely uneasy near a wooded edge. Cooper's hawks and other raptors certainly eat kestrels, and this may explain the behavior. Whatever the reason, kestrels are sometimes unwilling (even when hungry) to fly to the falconer near a stand of trees. This confounds many first-timers with what seems to be a serious "setback" in training. To be safe, always train and fly your kestrel in an open area, devoid of dense stands of trees.

VII EQUIPMENT

Kestrels are not difficult to house and maintain if provided the proper equipment. Plan to keep your kestrel tethered to a perch indoors at least during the hunting season. A hunting kestrel benefits from the controlled environment that this arrangement affords. Air temperature and physical activity (two principle variables in weight control) are moderated and the greater socialization with the falconer has obvious advantages.

The alternative of free lofting may seem easier, but it poses serious management problems. A loose kestrel at hunting weight frequently flies and runs about its enclosure, burning precious calories and risking injury. Such activity in a small space wears down flight feathers and talons and may bruise the bottom of the kestrel's feet. Free lofting should only be considered if the kestrel has suffered leg scale or other injury that precludes tethering.

Longwing block perches are often gorgeous works of art, but perching a kestrel on a block is to choose form over function. The combination of a kestrel's lightweight equipment and its habit of spinning on the perch poses a dangerous and unnecessary risk of entanglement. Under no circumstances should blocks be used as the kestrel's permanent home. For this use, the bow perch is superior. Indoor, weighted bows are simple to make, easy to clean and offer little opportunity for leash hang-ups.

My kestrel's bow perch is five inches high at the apex and welded to a steel harrow disk about fourteen inches in diameter. A patch of stadium-quality synthetic turf (Astroturf™) covers no more than three inches of the bow and is attached with small cable ties. A high quality turf is important, as kestrels will shred almost anything else. The small patch of turf provides enough space for a kestrel's feet while allowing the perch ring to slide easily.

The ring should be light and at least three inches in diameter. Some key rings fit this description and can be used safely once the open ends have been taped shut. I attach a permanent, four-inch leash to the ring with a simple fisherman's knot. The leash may be elastic (mine is), but elasticity is of uncertain value. In fact, some falconers cite elastic leashes as a possible cause of leg injury. Whatever material you use, the leash should be short and somewhat stiff to discourage entanglement.

The swivel system consists of three small ball-bearing swivels connected by a tiny split ring. On the ends of two swivels are placed jess clips (available as "lanyard hooks" at some hobby stores) and the leash is tied permanently to the third swivel. The holes in the four-inch long jesses need only be pin pricks to accommodate these small clips.

I make wide (3/4 inch) anklets to cover almost the entire tarsi. This may distribute the shock of a bate over a greater surface area and diminish leg scale damage. However, Jennifer Coulson disagrees with me; she suggests that wide jesses may actually abrade a larger area, so her preference is for more narrow anklets (1/2 inch). One clear advantage of the narrow anklet is that the kestrel's leg scales can be easily checked for injury. You may wish to experiment with both styles.

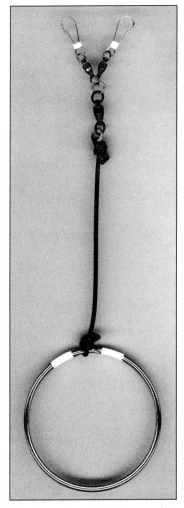

Tethering system @ 50% actual size.

A soft, thin but durable leather (such as kangaroo hide) makes excellent material for anklets and jesses. Before jessing a new kestrel, I apply a small amount of moisturizing cream to each of the kestrel's legs to reduce friction; leg scale damage is a real danger in the first few days of manning.

I use two lures, one for training and another for hunting. The training lure is introduced first. It weighs about 90 grams and is designed to discourage initial attempts at carrying. It is always presented on the ground. The hunting lure weighs only 30 grams, is soft and may be caught in the air by the kestrel without injury to its feet.

Jennifer Coulson prefers introducing the lure with a whole starling wing attached to it. This encourages interest in the unfamiliar lure and offers an immediate reward for binding to it. However, I soon switch to small tidbits tied or clipped to the lure. Eventually, intermittent reward on the glove after returning to the lure is sufficient to keep a kestrel's interest.

Some falconers do not use a glove when flying kestrels. Nonetheless, small hawks are more comfortable feeding on and returning to a secure perch. Bare skin tends to slide around beneath their feet, and although kestrels' feet are small, they have a firm grip and needle-sharp talons—something to consider.

Hoods are convenient tools but can be problematic with kestrels. They must fit perfectly and be literally light as feathers if they are to be useful. This perfection does not come easily; and if you are unskilled at making your own hoods, it does not come cheap. I am fortunate to have a friend in Eric Edwards, an excellent falconer and fine hood maker.

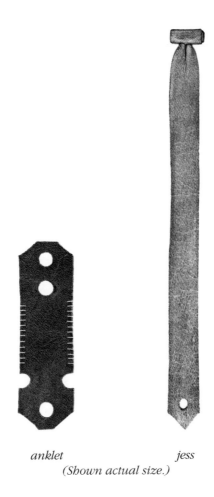

anklet   jess
(Shown actual size.)

Eric made countless hoods for my kestrels and countless adjustments to them at my request. Even so, few fit perfectly and none proved impossible for the kestrels to remove. (See Appendix #5/page 134.)

A far better solution is the humble hawk box, or "giant hood," as it is sometimes known. The construction is of lightweight wood paneling or thin plastic, reinforced with a frame of wooden quarter rounds.

The hawk box is invaluable for transporting kestrels, especially when larger hawks are in close quarters. Many kestrels fear even the sight of other raptors (particularly buteos) and the dark interior of a box has a calming effect. Kestrels should be introduced to the box within the first week of training. Provided the kestrel sits calmly inside, the box should become the kestrel's main form of transport.

Some radio transmitters are now small enough to be worn by kestrels. I have seen a neck-mounted, two-gram transmitter used without negative effect on a jack merlin, so it seems the added weight is not necessarily an impediment. But I don't recommend bells of any size, as these will only alert the quarry to the otherwise stealthy approach of a hunting kestrel.

Avoid electronic scales, since current models of comparable price to a triple-beam balance are not sufficiently accurate. Accuracy to one-tenth of one gram is required for the management of kestrels. The Ohaus "Dial-o-Gram" triple-beam balance is recommended.

Kestrel in hawk box.
9" wide x 14" high x 14" deep"
Perch is 5" from front & 5" up from bottom.

Female American kestrel on indoor bow perch.

VIII *WEATHERING*

Sunlight, fresh air and water are important to the health of trained raptors. Those that have regular exposure to the elements seem to maintain especially healthy plumage and skin color. Trained hawks are traditionally weathered on outdoor perches adjacent to a fresh bath. This system has worked well for centuries, compensating perhaps for the traditional dark and covered mews.

Despite the listed benefits, I feel that "formal" weathering of this kind is not suitable for kestrels. In fact, these benefits are far overshadowed by the dangers outdoor weathering poses to small raptors. Unlike larger hawks, kestrels are vulnerable to virtually every predator that may encounter them. Cats, dogs and raptors of every species are capable of killing perched kestrels. Leave a perched kestrel unattended and disaster will eventually result.

Even without the threat of predators, kestrels left in the weathering yard may injure themselves. They seem aware of their vulnerability when restrained near the ground and in the open. Many will bate constantly with leg scale and feather damage as possible results. I've seen kestrels at several field meets left bating and screaming at their perches; often, these small hawks are in the company of numerous other larger trained hawks, the presence of which must only add to the kestrels' agitation.

Female kestrel on bow perch in the home.

A simple solution to this problem is to "weather" the kestrel indoors or on a screened-in porch. Kestrels kept indoors on a bow perch may easily be placed in morning or evening sunlight and offered a bath. I keep a spare bow perch and plastic bath pan near the glass doors in my living room for this purpose. Several times a week, sunlight and schedule permitting, the kestrel will be allowed to bathe and preen for an hour before or after hunting. This practice, along with daily hunting, seems adequate to provide for a kestrel's weathering needs.

Weathering

Wild trapped female in adult plumage (Dexter), with a great tailed grackle, flown by Jonathan Millican. 46 birds in 40 days of hunting at time of photograph.

IX ENTERING

Eventually the kestrel must be introduced to the quarry it is intended to hunt. The most expedient method relies on the presentation of live quarry under circumstances overwhelmingly favorable to the kestrel's success. The process is known as "bagging." This contrived hunting experience boosts confidence in young predators, but it is also a potential source of emotional opposition to falconry. If practiced, it should be with extreme discretion—and in private.

Eyas kestrels may need numerous bagged starlings and sparrows before they show interest in wild quarry. However the experienced passage and haggard kestrels are more easily entered. A trained and hungry passage kestrel will usually bind to the first bagged starling it is offered; few will refuse a sparrow under any circumstance. For passagers, bagging is more an exercise in anti-carrying training than in entering.

It may be possible to enter a kestrel without the use of bagged quarry. Repeated slips at young sparrows or at birds roosting in a barn would eventually provide a kill. This "natural" approach is certainly more appealing, and I am tempted to recommend it over the use of bagged quarry. However, the risk of a passage kestrel carrying its first kill (especially a sparrow) is high; for this reason, I advise entering kestrels to a tethered starling. This approach has two advantages: it encourages a kestrel to view blackbirds on the ground as potential quarry and it provides a safe opportunity to practice making-in.

There are other ways to hunt with a kestrel, but slipping from a vehicle provides the greatest chance of early success. With this scenario in mind, the bagged starling should be presented in a way closely resembling a car slip; tether the quarry in short grass, away from cover or trees and fifteen or twenty feet from the roadside. It is not necessary to use more than six inches of line when tethering the starling.

The notion that bagged quarry should challenge the raptor is misplaced with regard to this form of falconry. If used at all, hindered quarry should be obvious to the kestrel and easy to subdue. Overwhelming success at bagged birds builds confidence, speeds entering to wild quarry and so reduces the need for further baggies.

Slip the kestrel from the driver's side window once it has seen and recognized the tethered bird. So long as it shows interest, it is not necessary to wait for the kestrel to fly on its own accord; a gentle toss is sometimes required to get a kestrel on the wing toward the first kill.

After the kestrel binds to the starling, make-in as quickly as possible to dispatch the tethered bird. This is most humane and also reduces the risk of injury to the kestrel. Allow the kestrel a few bites of breast meat, tid-bitting from the hand and whistling between bites to reinforce the association. Once it has eaten approximately a quarter crop (or about five grams) from the kill, offer a tiring on the glove and pull the starling away discretely.

Entering

The above describes an ideal entering. Not all will go so smoothly. Some kestrels will be reluctant to hold a tethered starling once having bound to it; others can hardly be removed from their kill knowing full well that a tiring is a fool's trade. However events unfold for you, remember that entering is best kept simple—the kestrel needs only to come away from the experience with confidence in its ability to catch and kill a bird.

As soon as the kestrel will bate at and bind to bagged quarry without hesitation, it is ready to fly at wild quarry. But it is vital that the first slips you choose be good ones. Buoyed by the easy success on bagged quarry, the kestrel may seem willing to attack birds at any distance. However, unless the slip is a close one, it is likely to fail. Early failures can break confidence, so make the first slips short and fly only at those birds the kestrel seems eager to catch.

X WEIGHT CONTROL

Weight control is the most important and challenging aspect of falconry with kestrels. Succeed here and you will find the larger hawks easy to maintain by comparison.

An average red-tailed hawk may weigh a thousand grams, ten times the size of an average kestrel. In contrast to the larger hawk, a hunting kestrel's response weight spans only two or three grams. In fact, most will require maintenance within a single gram. Managing a small hawk's food intake so precisely as to meet this daily target is not an easy skill to learn. (See Appendix 4/pg 133)

So goes the customary disclaimer, at any rate. In principle, weight management is a simple matter of arithmetic. With attention to detail and a delicate touch, most anyone can master it.

The first prerequisite to precision weight control is indoor housing. The daily rise and fall of outside temperatures make meeting a kestrel's target weight impossible. Even here in balmy Baton Rouge, I would not attempt to keep a hunting kestrel in an outdoor enclosure. However, when kept in a climate-controlled environment and fed a consistently high quality diet, kestrels will lose weight predictably.

A predictable hourly rate of weight loss is essential to weight control. Establishing this rate requires frequent and accurate measurement of the kestrel's food intake and body mass. Weigh newly trapped kestrels as often as six times a day for the first two weeks. Keep a chart near your gram-scale to record the time, date and the kestrel's body mass before and after each feeding. Put most simply, the rate of weight loss is calculated by dividing the number of grams lost between feedings by the number of hours between feedings.

With this information, it is possible to predict the number of grams a kestrel will lose between any two hours in a day. In theory, a trained kestrel can be fed enough at the end of each day to ensure that it will be again "on weight" for the next day's hunt. In practice, small adjustments may sometimes be necessary—a tidbit or two in the morning perhaps—but the goal is a kestrel precisely on hunting weight each day at the appointed time.

The following illustrates a typical day of weight control with a hunting kestrel:

A passage male, flying at 84 grams at 5:00 in the afternoon, killed a starling in a short flight. He was fed the starling's head at the site of the kill, then placed in his carry box while the other hawks had their turn. Back home near the scale, he was fed the quarry's heart, lungs, both legs and a portion of breast meat: a fairly good crop that boosted his weight to 98 grams at 7:00 p.m. The kestrel is now fourteen grams over hunting weight.

By 10:00 p.m. the kestrel dropped a gram. While sleeping, he dropped seven more to an 8:00 a.m. weight of 90 grams. That's eight grams lost in thirteen hours overnight.

> *By noon he will cast a pellet and will have dropped another three grams; by 5:00 p.m., he will be back at (or within half a gram of) the previous evening's hunting weight. That makes a total of six grams lost in nine hours of daylight.*

Weight loss during the day tends to be greater than at night, perhaps due to greater activity (preening, bathing, bating) in daylight hours. For practical purposes, the daily rate of weight loss is calculated as an average of day and nighttime losses. Over a 22-hour period, this kestrel lost a total of fourteen grams, or a little more than half a gram an hour (.6 gph). This rate of weight loss (.4–.6 gph) is normal for a healthy, hunting kestrel. (For the original theory of "22-hour weight control" I am indebted to Harry McElroy's writings and personal communication.)

Factors that increase the rate of weight loss include illness, low quality diet (chicken or washed meat), cold temperatures, additional exercise (such as repeated jumps to the fist) or failure to sleep. Factors that slow the rate include rich foods (dove or pigeon), overfeeding, warm temperatures and sleep.

Kestrels may accidentally be fed too much food in a single sitting, or conversely, an insufficient amount to carry them through the 22-hour cycle. Of these mistakes, the former is more immediately dangerous, as kestrels will occasionally become seriously ill from episodes of overfeeding (see "sour crop" in the chapter Accident and Illness).

Feeding too little in the evening, on the other hand, may be rectified in the morning by supplemental tidbits. Of course, missing a meal altogether will almost always result in disaster. Unlike the red-tailed hawk, a hunting kestrel can't skip a single meal without suffering steep, accelerated weight loss; should this occur at the low ebb of the cycle, it may cause the death of the kestrel.

The relationship between weight control and maintaining a tame passage kestrel is a close one. The passage male in the example above, tame as he was when at hunting weight, would bate violently away from me when kept even 10% above this weight for two consecutive days. Other kestrels may behave in this way on almost a daily basis in the hours after feeding. However, as the appointed hunting time grows near, most regain their fondness for the falconer.

Weight Control

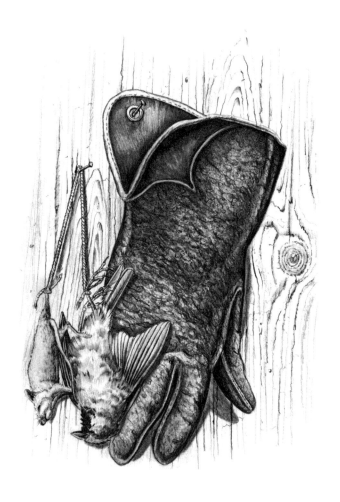

XI *DIET*

This section follows a discussion of weight control because the two factors are closely related. A high-quality diet is essential to any raptor being managed through a manipulation of body weight. Whenever food quantity is reduced, its quality must be excellent.

For all stages of a kestrel's captive management, its diet should consist of freshly killed, whole small birds and mice. Particularly good (and conveniently so from a hunting standpoint) are starlings and house sparrows. The flesh of these birds is sustaining and palatable, without unduly slowing digestion and normal weight loss. Of slightly lesser value are these same items frozen and thawed. Small portions of rabbit, squirrel, chicken heart, cockerels ("day-olds"), or even insects can be used temporarily if nothing better can be provided.

Of almost no value and indeed potentially harmful are white-meat chicken, hoof-stock of any kind or cut and spoiled (or freezer-burned) food. Obviously, road kills and processed meats are out of the question.

Haggard male kestrel with mouse.

Diet

Some believe that no small hawk should be taken for falconry unless small wild birds can be provided for its daily meal. There is merit to this. Fortunately, a hunting kestrel can provide such a diet for itself. Once entered and regularly taking quarry, the kestrel may be fed its daily ration from fresh kills and have the remainder frozen for later.

Until the kestrel is hunting on its own, however, it will be necessary to have quality food available in reserve. As training time will vary, I recommend that a falconer have at least twenty frozen starlings and a supply of fresh mice available before trapping a passage kestrel. This might be a good time to dust off the old air rifle!

XII *METHODS OF HUNTING*

To see a sparrow hawk (American kestrel) *strike a bird at rest on the ground is a wonderful sight, but the act is so rapid that "ere a man hath power to say, Behold" it is over. The present is obliterated; we look on something which is past. A long straight swoop, a flash of wings and the hawk is off with its prey ... It seems remarkable that so small a hawk should be able to vanquish a bird so nearly its own size, but I can attest that it does so occasionally, for I saw a sparrow hawk carry a starling in its talons to the roof of a building, where, standing on the dead body, the hawk tore it to pieces.*

Arthur C Bent, 1938
Life Histories of North American Birds of Prey

Slipping your kestrel at starlings as they forage along the roadside may be the easiest method of scoring a kill. Kestrels flown in this way become extremely proficient at catching birds, particularly with a close slip. Seasons totaling over 100 starlings are not difficult to achieve with this method—a dedicated "road warrior" will find 200 kills not an impossible goal.

While racking up on roadside starlings is undeniably fun, neither you nor your kestrel should be limited to this. The variety of possible hunting styles is surprising. Distant birds descending to feed may be flown from the fist in a long, low-altitude ambush flight commonly used by merlins and small accipiters. I have seen trained kestrels take successful slips at blackbirds so distant the flock appears only as a dark and swirling mass on the horizon. I've watched wild kestrels employ the same tactic on such birds as dove, meadowlarks and killdeer. In fact, long-distance ambush flights are probably the norm among those kestrels that catch larger birds in the wild.

Another style, one as engaging and participatory as rabbit hawking with a red-tailed hawk, is the pursuit of English sparrows in thick, isolated cover. Artificial cover provided by packing crates and farm machinery is ideal. Congregating sparrows may be chased from the fist or an elevated perch, either flushed by the falconer or pursued in an opportunistic fashion by the kestrel. If sparrow densities are high, kestrels will often take a stand in cover and ambush them, sometimes chasing them down on foot. When hawking wooden packing pallets with an experienced kestrel, it may be slipped inside like a ferret and will search each level while you stand by to prevent the sparrows' escape. Once a kill is made, simply reach into the stack and remove kestrel and quarry together!

English sparrows are in some ways the perfect quarry: they are reluctant to leave cover, can be flushed singly across open ground and will put-in if pursued vigorously. You will find that these small birds provide some of the best flights possible with a kestrel, and that they inspire the sort of determined, reckless pursuit that one might expect of an accipiter. The aid of a dog for pointing and flushing is a surprisingly useful addition to sparrow hawking, and as my whippet will eagerly attest, any sort of dog may be employed with good results.

Flying kestrels in a cast can be very effective. Historically, the desert longwings (lanners, luggars and sakers) have been flown together in direct pursuit flights that seem to bring out the best in each cast member. Perhaps this is another way in which the American kestrel may resemble others of this group.

One season, a friend and I flew our passage kestrels (a male and female) together on a regular basis. After a brief period of acclimation, we were treated to some very surprising and exciting falconry. Large flocks of starlings would generally yield two birds taken simultaneously and thus double the effectiveness of each slip. On dual flights at single birds, two kestrels in pursuit proved capable of meeting each dodge with a new attack and were thus frequently successful. Some of the most surprising catches were of birds that mobbed one kestrel on a kill and so were taken by the other with a late slip.

For any two falconers flying kestrels in the same town, flying in a cast is definitely something I would recommend. It may be that passage kestrels, each well-entered beforehand, have the best chance of succeeding as a team. Several combinations of my own passage kestrels have flown well together. On the occasions that we've tried to pair passage kestrels with an eyas, the teamwork disintegrated. However, it is noteworthy that no combination of kestrels resulted in aggression on kills or on the wing. Sadly, back home on perches the situation can be different (see the chapter on Accident and Illness for more detail).

American Kestrels in Modern Falconry

I've had two kestrels, both eyases, which learned to wait-on if provided a cold day and a little wind. The first was encouraged to do so by repeatedly tossing starlings to him in an open field, a method similar to that used with larger longwings. The second was trained to stoop the lure and later encouraged to wait-on by occasionally hiding the lure between passes. Both kestrels would hold a pitch of approximately 100 feet and remain in position for several minutes. Both kestrels would actively stoop at and chase sparrows flushed beneath them, but this proved the least successful method of catching quarry with either.

Other falconers have had genuine, repeated success training their kestrels to wait-on. Where large numbers of English sparrows exist in natural field environments, this must be the most spectacular method of catching them with a kestrel. Oregon falconers Greg and Mary Griswold have had more success at this than most. Mary writes:

> *On flying kestrels from a soar instead of fist or perch: the key, we've found, is to treat them like any other falcon. If you follow the old wives' tales and believe they can't—well, they won't. We expect the kestrels we fly to hunt from a height of at least 100 feet, using lots of bagged sparrows (hand released, not tethered) during the training process and not rewarding them when they sit somewhere, waiting for an easy meal. Once the birds were manned and trustworthy (for the most part), we flew them at fairly high weights.*

> *Greg flew a tiercel Kestrel (Kit) as a first-year novice. Kit weighed approximately 93 grams at trapping, in September, and we ultimately flew him the few months before release the following March at about 140 grams.*

Methods of Hunting

I flew both a tiercel (Duggan) and a falcon (Lacey). Duggan's trapping weight was similar to Kit's. Lacey was trapped in October at a weight of about 112 grams.

The falcons seem to be a little less aerial than the tiercels, but all will wait-on with the proper training. We flew all three kestrels on nothing but feathered game. In our area, that means English sparrows. I couldn't possibly remember numbers taken, but we took enough to keep both us and the birds interested in the game.

A few of my kestrels, and those of other falconers, have taken dove and quail. Wild kestrels do take these quarries, though it is probably not common. I consider these kills exceptional. Trained kestrels readily attack doves in low altitude ambush flights, but being small-footed they seem unable to hold on to them easily. Mourning doves have famously loose plumage; the most common end to dove flights finds the kestrel on the ground clutching a pile of gray feathers. After many such attempts (few successful), my kestrels have eventually lost interest in doves.

The only quail I have taken were chased into a shed by an eyas female and literally run down in lengths of PVC pipe. While certainly entertaining, this was not a situation I could hope to duplicate often.

Snipe can be taken by surprise, but probably not otherwise.

One possible scenario that could bring these exceptional quarries into the realm of the catchable is the combination of waiting-on flights and a pointing dog. To my knowledge, this has never been attempted. Perhaps the pinnacle of kestrel falconry awaits us? Until then, for regular success with a trained kestrel, I suggest hawking starlings and English sparrows by the following methods.

Roadside Hawking

Slipping a kestrel from an automobile will provide two important advantages: instant speed (5–20 mph) and the element of surprise. Moreover, the increased mobility allows the falconer more opportunities when hawking and thus betters the chances at success for each outing.

Though "road-hawking" may seem like a new twist in falconry, records of its employment go back several decades. Indeed, the automobile merely replaced the formerly conventional hawking vehicle, the horse, in the ancient sport of flying longwings "out of the hood" at rooks and other corvids. Similarly, the falconers of the Middle East have replaced their trusty camels with convertible Range Rovers for pursuit flights at the houbara.

While the kestrel's greatest aesthetic potential might be found in long distance ambushes or waiting-on flights, clearly its greatest utilitarian potential lies along the roadside. For putting hawk food in the freezer, there's simply no substitute for "dinking" starlings in the park on Sunday morning. With a kestrel amply conditioned to this flight, three or four starlings can be taken during any given outing. Eight starlings or more are possible on a particularly gluttonous occasion. This fact has been proven not only with kestrels, but with just about every hawk physically small enough to fit through a car window.

Though stockpiling starlings in this fashion may seem unsporting, in practice such scores reflect more the road-hawker's greater access to slips than the ease with which quarry is caught by this method. Measured in flights per kill, a kestrel's average success at roadside birds is similar to that of a red-tailed hawk hunting rabbits in the field: one flight in four resulting in a kill.

Yet few days are average. Any hunt can feature "runs," where nearly every starling flown is caught, as well as "slumps," where birds are repeatedly missed regardless of circumstance. The trick to success in roadside hawking lies in anticipating

"Sally" slicked down and ready for a slip at a house sparrow.

these apparent lapses in confidence, then avoiding them by offering the kestrel closer slips at a favored quarry. When confidence is high, go for long shots or otherwise difficult quarry and when confidence ebbs start slipping at "gimmes."

To remove a kestrel from successive kills without upsetting it is not difficult. The first objective is to center the attention on one part of the quarry so that it is not randomly footing the bird at every angle. I usually pull the skin away from the neck and head of the dead starling, then allow the kestrel to feed from there. While the kestrel is eating the head, I maneuver the body of the bird into my gloved palm and out of sight. With so small a target, the feeding kestrel will normally release the bird to place both feet on the glove for leverage.

I allow the kestrel a few good bites then simply pull the bird down from underneath and slip it into the quarry bag. If it needs to eat a bit more, it is convenient to slip a starling leg in between my fingers and pull the quarry away while the kestrel is working on this tiring.

"Phoebe" about to catch a sparrow in Amarillo, Texas.

Methods of Hunting

A word of caution: road-hawking in areas of heavy auto or pedestrian traffic can be hazardous to all involved. Early morning and late evening hunts, often convenient from the falconer's standpoint, have the added advantage of being less fraught with potential traffic dangers. Sunday morning hunts are jewels. Also, it is preferable to hunt in open, remote locations such as industrial parks, ball fields, community college campuses and the like. Not only will more dramatic flights be had in these open spaces, the neighborhood dangers of Cooper's hawks, cats, dogs and cars are greatly reduced.

Pallet Hawking

Packing pallets are the square wooden platforms used to support cargo for lifting and transport. Stacks of these platforms are commonly kept near the loading docks of supermarkets, farmer's markets and chain stores, where they provide good roosting habitat for resident flocks of English sparrows.

I first tried hawking sparrows in this situation in the summer of 1990, when attempting to enter an inexperienced eyas female kestrel. Having found a loading dock with both pallets and house sparrows, I slipped the kestrel into the pallet stack and began to rattle the surrounding structure. As soon as the sparrows began to move, the kestrel launched a series of brief attacks, dashing after birds that passed her position. Within minutes this approach proved successful and the kestrel had her first wild kill.

On subsequent hunts my kestrel grew bolder, often stalking sparrows on her own while I stood by watching. Each platform level would be carefully searched on foot, with the kestrel pausing occasionally to listen and peer through the cracks at anxious sparrows. With my aid in keeping the sparrows from escaping, they could be cornered and caught by the kestrel with ease.

I have flown five of my tamest kestrels in this manner, each of which learned the technique quickly and enjoyed regular success. The other kestrels would carry small birds and could not be flown at them without risk. For those more reliable kestrels, sparrow hawking offered a welcome respite from "drive-by falconry" and an opportunity to involve friends and dogs in the hunt.

Of course, packing pallets are not the only sparrow hangouts that can be raided by trained kestrels and their entourage: warehouses, barns, silos, shopping malls, feed lots and landscape shrubbery all provide adequate roosting places for these birds and unique opportunities to fly them. And in such locations, not all kills will take place in cover—kestrels will stoop readily from a rooftop or lamppost and can catch sparrows on the wing.

When flushing house sparrows for the kestrel, position is paramount. Kestrels lack the explosive acceleration of a small accipiter, so even close flushes are more likely to lead to tail chases rather than a fast midair catch. In most situations, it is more effective to flush sparrows toward a perched kestrel than to flush them away from her. Ideally, a fence or hedgerow will end beneath some tall perch—a telephone pole or the corner of a building. House sparrows found congregating at one end of the hedge can be "shuffled" toward the kestrel if care is taken not to frighten them too badly; a gentle tap on one end of the hedge is all that is necessary. If not flushed straight away from the hedge, small groups of sparrows are likely to flit down to the end farthest from the falconer. The sight of these birds fluttering into cover beneath the kestrel should prove irresistible, and the advantage of a direct vertical stoop is just what it needs to catch one. Sparrows can be shuffled toward a kestrel under a variety of circumstances; taking note of good potential slips around town will pay dividends throughout the season.

Night Roost Hawking

Another method of hawking starlings and sparrows with a kestrel is to fly them at their nighttime roosts. The first time I saw this technique employed was by a wild kestrel and I have witnessed several others do it since.

Evening raids on roosting birds and rising bats are probably more common than officially recorded. As darkness approaches and starlings swirl in for the night, small raptors are often in attendance to take advantage. I've seen Cooper's hawks, sharp-shins and kestrels snatch birds from flocks in flight or follow singles into buildings and catch them inside. One particularly bold male kestrel took starlings from the open beams of a radio tower, tumbling with these birds to the ground below.

Both starlings and house sparrows roost communally—a fact that many warehouse and shopping mall owners deeply regret! These large avian congregations can make for noisy, messy and most unwelcome tenants. Securing landowner permission to hunt them with a kestrel or other small hawk is usually easy. With the aid of a strong flashlight, or the facility's own lighting system, roosting starlings and sparrows can be taken readily with kestrels. Bring along a larger hawk (especially a Cooper's or male Harris') and the pigeons will be in serious trouble as well.

Starlings roost most frequently in buildings or roadside billboards and sparrows more commonly in dense trees or tall shrubs. However, I have found both species roosting in a variety of locations, so no strict rules apply. You may find their roosts simply by driving through suburban or industrial areas in late evening, keeping eyes and ears alert for swarming flocks piling in for the night. Also, a daytime check for sparrow and starling mutes beneath likely cover will often give them away.

Well-entered falconry kestrels are surprisingly easy to introduce to hawking at night. I've flown hawks of five different species in this manner, all of which were soon successful. The main requirement of the novice "roost-hawk" is that it be precisely at the normal daytime hunting weight, and that it returns immediately when called. Simply shining the flashlight on the garnished fist is sufficient to call most hawks back at night, but it's best to insist on prompt response. Flying well after dark (rather than at dusk) reduces the hawk's natural tendency to look for a roosting spot of its own. Even the Cooper's hawk, infamous for getting the "evening jitters," can fly with perfect reliability once full darkness sets in.

Before beginning a kestrel's moonlighting career, catch at least a dozen birds by more conventional methods. Then, choose a starling roost near an ample ambient light source (street lamps or floodlights), where passersby are unlikely distractions. A fenced, private warehousing facility is ideal. With luck, starlings will be roosting on a low rafter or support beam just a few feet above your head. By shining a bright flashlight on the nearest of these, the kestrel should soon recognize its favorite dish and dash into the rafters to catch it.

Ideally, the kestrel will both bind to a starling and bring it to the ground, or miss altogether and simply sit tight in the rafters. In the latter case, you will have an opportunity to practice calling the kestrel to your illuminated fist. In the former, make-in to the struggling kestrel quickly. Be sure to keep the flashlight trained on your kestrel, so that it may see well enough to effectively control the starling.

Should the starling flee to another beam or to the open night sky, the kestrel will probably pursue it. Try not to panic as your kestrel disappears into the dark; it will not likely go far. A tail-chase may sometimes be aborted by removing the flashlight beam from the starling being pursued. However, early flights should be kept short, with repeated calling to the fist to establish this as habit.

Soon your kestrel will understand where the quarry is hiding and will follow the flashlight beam with intense interest. Once this behavior is established, you may find that the kestrel bates at any shiny, eye-ball-sized object such as a rivet or bolt in the rafters above! You may also notice how well kestrels can see in low light conditions, as it bates toward darkened rafters at birds you had not seen.

Though night-roost hawking may seem to invite disaster in the form of owl predation or loss, these dangers are minimized by flying the kestrel at hunting weight, demanding immediate response when called and taking close slips. Additionally, once the kestrel is well entered to this flight, it tends not to chase birds far but rather returns promptly for another slip.

 *CARRYING*

With sparrow hawking come inevitable opportunities for kestrels to carry. This vice would seem more common to passage and haggard birds, but there are circumstances under which even the tamest eyas hawks will be tempted to carry a fresh kill. Training to prevent this is best begun in the first two weeks of captivity and continued after the kestrel is on the creance.

A kestrel that will not allow the falconer to walk up to it on the perch is unlikely to allow him to do so on a sparrow. So, the first milestone of anti-carrying training is encouraging the kestrel to sit calmly as you walk toward it.

With passage kestrels, and perhaps most other non-imprinted longwings, tid-bitting is the key. Small morsels of meat offered consistently and repeatedly on the perch, the lure and bagged or wild quarry will ensure the kestrel looks forward to the approach of the falconer. Associating a particular word or whistle with each tidbit will soon cue the kestrel to look up expectantly when called. This behavior can circumvent attempts to carry if the call is given while making-in. Getting your hawk's attention in this way—even for a moment—can save the day.

Kestrels that lean toward the falconer for a handout while standing on a garnished lure are well on their way to safely hawking sparrows. Those that attempt to bolt with the lure or bagged quarry probably need more repetition, or a slight weight reduction, or both.

When approaching a nervous small hawk on a sparrow, observing a few basic rules may mean the difference between taking it home and leaving it out overnight.

First, relax: if the hawk did not snatch the sparrow and bolt immediately, it probably intends to eat on the spot or in nearby cover. Allow it a moment for composure, to pluck a few feathers and begin eating. Once it has broken in, approach casually and indirectly. If the kestrel stops eating to watch you, speak softly. This will often break the tension and encourage it to resume plucking. When only a few feet remain between yourself and the kestrel, crouch low, whistle and begin offering tidbits until it is safely on the fist. The kestrel should grow steadier with each kill, but it is wise to exercise caution on all small quarry:

Carrying

Bridget Bradshaw & passage female kestrel after flying to the kite.

XIV *EXERCISE & CONDITIONING*

While flying a friend's merlin on sparrows in open country, he and I observed a very persistent female kestrel joining the chase on several occasions. As birds flushed at our feet and the merlin took off in pursuit, the kestrel would launch her own attack from a nearby building. Typically she would take a position behind the merlin and attempt to catch the sparrows as they neared cover.

The kestrel was slower in the tail-chase and steadily lost ground to the merlin in direct pursuit. However, as the sparrows put-in, she matched the larger merlin turn for turn and on a few occasions beat the merlin to their quarry. Whichever individual proved the winner in these contests, no aggression or pirating was noted between them. The merlin caught and cached most of the sparrows; the kestrel simply returned to her perch to await the next chase.

This wild kestrel's relatively slow flight (compared to a merlin) and high maneuverability mirror my observations of trained kestrels. Where wild kestrels differ from most trained ones is in sheer stamina. The dual chases we observed covered hundreds of yards of open ground and continued for several minutes of hard flying each. This performance would continue with only short breaks between flights for as long as two hours. The stamina displayed by this wild kestrel exceeds anything I've seen in mine.

A trained kestrel may lack stamina because practical falconry slips are typically short. Over time, the combination of weight control and short slips may cause the kestrel to lose muscle tone, endurance and enthusiasm for longer flights.

To counter this, regular indoor exercise can be helpful. Place the kestrel on the ground at your feet and call it repeatedly to the fist (or to the top of a carry pole), elevating it as high as you can. Offer tidbits randomly between every three and six flights. This practice is commonly known as "jumping-up." Initial episodes of such exercise tend to exhaust my kestrels quickly; they are usually breathing hard after thirty jumps. But it takes only days to double this. Once the kestrel is capable of seventy or eighty jumps per session without fatigue, the endurance for long flights and speed in close quarters will noticeably improve. Fit kestrels will catch more birds and under more difficult circumstances.

Male kestrel & male (jack) merlin.

A much more dramatic technique for getting your kestrel fit is illustrated here by Washington state falconer Bridget Bradshaw in an excerpt from her article in the North American Falconers' Association newsletter Hawk Chalk (Vol. 40, no. 2; August, 2001):

After we trained Athena, she caught some wild birds, grasshoppers and worms, but flying to the kite is Athena's favorite exercise. We use a "Devotion to Motion" delta [wing] kite with a wingspan of eight feet and 600 feet of string. An alligator clip holds a tidbit (the back half of a small mouse) about ten feet below the kite. The tidbit of meat has to be loose enough in the clip so Athena can snatch it away but tight enough so it won't fall off before she grabs it.

I hold the kite while Dad unwinds some string. The stronger the wind, the less string you have to roll out. Then I toss the kite into the air and Dad runs. Athena will climb as high as the kite and pull the tidbit off the string. Sometimes it takes her ten minutes of hard work to circle all the way up to over our heads where the kite is flying. She is just a tiny speck in the sky at 600 feet.

Haggard female "Phoebe" feeding on starling.

XV *HAWKING YEAR-ROUND*

Spring comes early to southeastern Louisiana, bringing warm tropical weather, rain and the quick regeneration of foliage. Rabbit and squirrel hawking become increasingly difficult by late February. The "big hawks" are typically put-up before the molt and sometimes even before the close of hunting season.

Fortunately, the change of seasons need not effect your kestrel's hunting. In fact, spring and early summer are particularly good times to hawk starlings and house sparrows. These are the salad days for hunting unprotected small birds and they will provide the greatest bags of the season.

Longer days and warmer weather bring both starlings and house sparrows into breeding condition. This is a time of dedicated feeding in exposed locations—perfect for the kestrel's needs. This seasonal shift` in the quarry's behavior is quite a change from the nervous, unpredictable ways of winter flocks. Suddenly, these birds are found in small groups, spending hours each day tucked deep into the rich spring clover. What a beautiful sight this is! As friends Tom and Jennifer Coulson reflect, it is a vision too few can fully appreciate.

After a winter making the most of difficult slips on large, wary flocks, the kestrel will find spring birds easy to catch. There are good reasons to take advantage of this: extra food can be put away to feed the kestrel during the molt, eyas raptors can be provided a fresh and varied diet at little cost and bagged starlings can be easily provided to the young hawks as they mature. Finally, longer days allow the falconer more opportunity to hunt after work—a welcome change from the hectic winter hawking schedule.

My kestrels generally start molting in May or June and finish by the end of September. This gives one a long hawking season even if the kestrel is not flown during the molt. However, kestrels can be flown successfully throughout the summer. My practice has been to fly on a reduced schedule: the kestrels are kept three or four grams above hunting weight on days not flown (a considerable amount for a kestrel) and dropped back two or three times a week for late afternoon or early morning outings. Off-days are spent jumping the kestrel to the fist for daily meals.

I've found this a rewarding way to keep kestrels tame and conditioned over the summer without inflicting significant damage to new feathers. Regular exercise and fresh food are added benefits of this off-season regime.

If summer hawking doesn't appeal to you, note that kestrels do molt more quickly when not flown and will return to hunting condition without difficulty in the fall.

Jonathan Wood's male kestrel and European starling.

 *ACCIDENT & ILLNESS*

All predators risk bodily injury when chasing and killing other animals. Trained kestrels, regularly capturing birds their own size, are no exception. Also, the consumption of fresh prey poses some risk of disease transmission to the predator; one might add to this category the danger of secondary poisoning from sources such as Avitrol (Holler, et. al., 1982), a chemical applied to bait grain that, according to the manufacturer (Avitrol Corporation), causes birds "to emit distress and alarm cries and visual displays," and on some species "may be used as an avicide." (from http://www.avitrol.com/)

Fortunately for trained hawks, these dangers are mitigated by the careful attentions of the falconer. Brian Millsap and I (1995) measured this benefit by comparing the mortality estimates of captive kestrels with those of wild birds. We found that trained kestrels suffer an annual mortality of 7.7%, which is dramatically lower than the estimated 67% first-year mortality recorded for their wild counterparts (Henny and Wight, 1972).

Contrary to conventional wisdom, kestrels are remarkably tough customers. My kestrels and others have survived numerous bizarre and unexpected mishaps, as well as a number of sadly preventable conditions. Thousands of cumulative hawking hours have proven these kestrels equal to what the world throws at them.

The following list includes the most common maladies suffered by trained kestrels in my experience. None of these need be fatal or crippling, but the potential for disaster is ever present. All small raptors require special attention to health and safety concerns.

Leg Scale Damage

Repetitive abrasion of the tarsi and toes from a jess or anklet can eventually ulcerate the affected skin and lead to serious complications. Scales may separate or be worn off, leaving the soft unprotected skin beneath them vulnerable to greater damage. Swelling and infection may be followed by necrosis and loss of digits in extreme cases. Any small areas of redness or swelling should be closely examined and treated before tissue is permanently damaged.

Prevention is by far the best policy with regard to these (and all other) injuries. Jesses of soft, thin leather, well oiled and flanged on all exposed edges will help to minimize damage. Recently trapped kestrels, tied to a perch and left alone unhooded, are at great risk of leg scale damage. Such kestrels will bate excessively and in short order begin to abrade toes and tarsi at all points of contact. A short leash and a precisely fitted hood or (better yet) a well-constructed hawk box are essential tools for the prevention of leg scale damage at the early stages of training.

If damage does occur, remove the jesses and apply antibiotic ointment to the affected area. See your veterinarian if the damage is serious. When caught at the early stages and quickly treated, jess-related abrasions can heal completely. Remember that having to treat these injuries before the kestrel is manned and trained will pose significant management problems, so avoid them at all cost.

Bumblefoot

This condition may sometimes arise from the same excessive bating that causes leg scale damage. However, smooth perching surfaces, bruising of the ball of the foot, talon puncture and even poor quality diet are all implicated in bumblefoot. The callous-like lesions tend to grow slowly on the pad of one or both feet and may swell with fluid or infection. If caught early, they may disappear after a change in husbandry. If left untreated, they will eventually cripple the raptor.

Preventive husbandry is simple and almost completely effective: a high quality diet, regular observation of the foot and the use of Astroturf on perching surfaces will together virtually eliminate bumblefoot as a concern.

Collision

Andrew Village's (1994) natural history of the Eurasian kestrel *(F. tinnunculus)* found collision to be a leading cause of mortality in the birds of his study. Kestrels are vulnerable to windows and automobiles, and the urban nature of starling and sparrow hawking brings these dangers to the fore. I have on several occasions recovered my kestrels after chasing birds into windows and fences, or being chased into them by crows or other antagonists. On one horrible afternoon, I had to recover an unconscious female that hit a passing car while chasing English sparrows.

Remarkably, none of these mishaps killed or permanently injured my kestrels. Even the female knocked unconscious soon awoke unharmed. But I've been lucky. Under no circumstances should the falconer slip a kestrel at birds near windows, cars, fences or any other obvious obstruction. All collisions are potentially fatal to small raptors.

Sour Crop

This is a serious condition whereby the food in a kestrel's crop grows septic with bacteria. It can kill the kestrel and probably accounts for the death of most of the small hawks that perish in captivity. Sour crop does not occur at random, but rather follows a predictable progression; the kestrel is generally low in weight and then overfed. This combination is deadly.

Although a "bulging crop" is often recommended as a reward for a trained kestrel's success on quarry, it should never be allowed to a small hawk at hunting weight. The most food a hunting kestrel should receive in any one sitting is that amount sufficient to carry it over for 22 hours (see the section on weight control for details). For a kestrel at hunting weight, this amount is likely to be between twelve and fifteen grams.

Should a kestrel develop sour crop, the falconer's action must be swift. Depending on the severity of the condition, a veterinarian or experienced falconer may have to remove the rotting food from the kestrel's crop and administer oral antibiotics. In less severe cases, or as a possible preventive measure after accidental overfeeding, I recommend offering water regularly from the fingertips and keeping the kestrel awake for several hours into the night to speed digestion.

Accident and Illness

Predation

Kestrels are vulnerable to a wide variety of larger predators. Under falconry management, this danger is reduced by the proximity of the falconer, but this protection is not always sufficient. I know of several cases of predation on trained kestrels; one killed by a red-shouldered hawk, one killed by a barred owl and another by a rat snake. Two of my kestrels and three others* flown by friends have been caught and carried away by Cooper's hawks. Though the kestrels were released with only minor injuries, the danger here is obvious.

Several house cats and small dogs have attempted to snatch my kestrels from kills while hawking in suburban settings. Trained kestrels may even fatally attack one another, as I unfortunately discovered after leaving an otherwise compatible pair too close in a darkened room.

Prevention of predation requires special vigilance on the part of the falconer. Flying at dusk or dawn or other conditions of poor visibility probably invites danger, as does flying near dense woodland. Falconers must assist their kestrels with quarry immediately, and never leave them alone on a kill. While a nearby human form may deter a wild predator, tame cats and dogs have no fear and will charge in literally between the falconer's legs. The best policy is to take close slips when hawking in tight areas and to recover the kestrel as soon as possible after each flight.

Our running and yelling in the direction of the fleeing Cooper's hawk saved all five kestrels. Should this happen to you, make every effort to pursue the hawk and save your bird; evidently, wild Cooper's hawks are easily spooked from would-be kills.

Coccidiosis

This disease is caused by a protozoan (Redig, 1994) contracted by kestrels that eat infected quarries. Kestrels may also re-infect themselves through contact with their own mutes. The symptoms with which I am most familiar include an initial increase in daily weight loss (while maintaining a good appetite), general fatigue after chasing quarry, and finally, the appearance of small crimson spots in the mutes. These spots are minute drops of blood emanating from intestinal tissue irritated by the organism.

I am not certain which prey birds are the most common carriers, but possibly all social, ground-feeding birds have the potential to spread the protozoan among themselves. As I almost always feed some of the fresh quarry to my kestrels, transmission of this organism is probably inevitable.

However, coccidiosis has not been a serious problem for my kestrels, even when it has reached an advanced stage. Though I still occasionally encounter this disease, I make no extraordinary effort to avoid it. The antibiotic "Albon" (sulfadimethoxine) given in oral suspension is effective, and regular changing of the paper beneath the bow perch reduces contact with mutes. (Consult your veterinarian for advice on the most current treatment options.) So long as my experience with coccidiosis remains benign, I will continue to feed fresh quarry to my hawks. The taste of fresh quarry is a great confidence booster to kestrels, and no food is more nutritious.

Accident and Illness

Cold Climate Concerns

Living and hawking in the southeast presents few cold weather concerns. I am much more familiar with the discomforts of hot weather hawking. However, a few trips to the Great Plains in winter have given me some empathy for falconers flying small hawks in such areas.

Most importantly, an increase in the quantity of food is recommended under conditions of extreme cold, but how much will depend upon the level of control the falconer enjoys over a hawk. If the kestrel will catch quarry and respond immediately five or six grams over normal hunting weight, I recommend the increase. If not, the falconer must respond to the kestrel's greater metabolic demands by feeding small portions at regular intervals throughout the day.

I stress the importance of maintaining control at all times, as this factor becomes critical in harsh and unfamiliar environments. The falconer may want to fly a kestrel heavier to ward off the cold, but if this means the hawk spends the night out for lack of control, then the purpose has been defeated.

The successful falconer will be in the habit of weighing a kestrel often, keeping it inside when not flying, and offering the highest quality food at all times. Such habits are never more important than when a kestrel is flown in cold climates.

Broken Feathers

Hardly a traumatic injury or dread disease, a broken feather is still an unpleasant and generally avoidable nuisance. A low, uncomplicated perching apparatus combined with enough leash to clear the tail in a bate should prevent the majority of feather problems. As cavity nesters, kestrels are equipped with elastic feather shafts that rarely suffer bad breaks. The occasional bent feather may be immersed for a few minutes in warm water and restored completely. Should a shaft split or tip bend so far that it creases, a dab of super-glue will generally hold the feather together until the end of the season.

Imping needles may be used on bad breaks, but finding suitable needles for such small feathers may be difficult. A more reliable method for smaller hawks is the "shaft-to-shaft" technique, where the broken feather is replaced completely with another by inserting the new shaft into the old just beneath the tail coverts. At the join, either the new or old feather may be split slightly to accommodate the other, and a small amount of adhesive applied to fill any gaps and seal the repair. A sleeve or patch may be affixed over the join for extra support, fashioned from a small square of shaft cut from a larger bird's feather.

Loss

Of all the small raptors flown for falconry, kestrels are probably the least frequently lost. Unlike accipiters, they do not sit motionless in cover on kills and indeed are rarely flown in cover thick enough to conceal them. Unlike merlins, they will rarely pursue quarry in a lengthy tail chase nor typically attack birds at great distances from the falconer. If unsuccessful on a slip, most kestrels simply fly up to the nearest pole or exposed branch and wait to be called down. The short range and conspicuous nature of trained kestrels make them relatively hard to lose under normal circumstances.

Still, I have ultimately lost several kestrels and occasionally left others out overnight. The circumstances surrounding these events are typical of those that might be expected of urban hawking. One caught a roosting starling in a billboard and could not be found the next morning. Another caught and ate a sparrow on a warehouse roof and could not be retrieved after several days' effort. One was chased by crows and disappeared into a summer thermal. Of those left out overnight, pursuit by crows, grackles or red-shouldered hawks typically preceded loss. In these cases, the kestrels were recovered in the immediate area where lost; I presume that they did not return when called because they did not wish to expose themselves. It is hard to blame a small hawk for hiding under these circumstances.

To prevent even temporary loss, weight control and lure training are important. Though a frightened kestrel may be reluctant to return, under no other circumstance should it hesitate when called. For the kestrel's safety and the protection of your investment in its training, it should always be flown at hunting weight and be well conditioned to the lure.

Eyas male "Beaumont" in first year plumage.

XVII SIGNS OF HEALTH

It may be helpful to describe the appearance and behavior of a kestrel in perfect health. The falconer should be able to assess the general condition of a charge by careful and regular inspection.

Feather Condition

Like the desert longwings, kestrels have soft plumage that generally lacks the high sheen or "bloom" of the peregrine and its close relatives. Nonetheless, a tame and healthy kestrel should preen daily, keeping all feathers in perfect order. Regular bathing is also a sign of good health, though passage and haggard kestrels are often reluctant to bathe in the first few weeks of captivity. In general, a fit kestrel will not allow soil, water or blood to mat feathers for more than a day.

Eyes

A kestrel's eyes should be round and alert during the day, frequently taking in their surroundings with a look of head-bobbing interest. A kestrel in low condition or fighting infection will often display an "oval-eyed" appearance with lids half-closed.

Feet, Tarsi and Cere

The exposed skin of the kestrel should have a light yellow to orange color. Newly trapped haggard birds may have particularly deep orange coloration, which may fade normally in captivity. However, a pale gray or light blue cast to the skin is a sign of ill health and probably due to a low-quality diet. Fresh, whole small birds and mammals should be offered daily and will quickly improve the kestrel's skin color.

Check frequently for signs of scale damage, redness or swelling of the feet and tarsi. Bumblefoot and scale separation are both serious maladies most successfully treated in their early stages.

Mutes

A healthy kestrel will produce a variety of normal mute types, which may be observed to change throughout the day. If well fed the previous night, the first mute in the morning is generally large, somewhat watery, with a well-formed fecal component. As the hours pass, the mutes will become smaller and consist of dark fecal matter surrounded by white urates. Immediately before hunting time, the fecal matter may contain a slight greenish tint. If fed on a fresh, bloody kill, the kestrel's following few mutes may have a frothy, dark brown consistency. Later, as the meat is digested, this will change to the more typical black and white type and will be produced in relatively large quantities over the next couple of hours.

Regular excretion is a sign that the kestrel's digestive system is in good working order; one early symptom of sour crop is the kestrel's failure to mute within an hour of a large feeding. Large, slick black mutes, often accompanied by a foul odor, are signs that the it is suffering from some digestive distress, possibly due to infection, toxin or spoiled food.

Casting

A healthy kestrel fed whole small animals (including bone with fur or feathers) will cast a small pellet each morning. This pellet should be round and compact, without a strong odor. Though healthy kestrels sometimes fail to cast daily, this can be a sign of an impacted crop if it persists for more than two days. Kestrels will sometimes swallow small indigestible items (pieces of rug, leather, paper, etc.) that can block the crop and lead to serious complications if not cast. It is imperative that the kestrel's immediate environment contain no such dangerous items and that normal casting material (fur and feathers) be offered regularly.

That "Healthy" Look

Finally, a healthy kestrel will often sit with its feathers puffed out to the extent that they make it appear almost totally round. In a larger hawk, this might indicate serious illness or low condition. In a kestrel, it is often a sign of well-adjusted contentment—provided it is not accompanied by obvious symptoms of disease.

A healthy kestrel at rest will stand on one foot, without seeming to favor either. It may preen occasionally, perhaps concentrating on a single feather in particular need of attention. Its wings will be held up against the body, with their tips crossing near the center of the tail. Occasionally, it will engage in a languid stretching of one or both wings, dropping them slowly beneath the perch until fully extended. This is the look of a kestrel in the fit of health, recently home from the field and digesting the "fruit" of its labor.

Passage female "Ella."

Signs of Health

Passage male "Tycho" in adult plumage.

XVIII *THE FUTURE*

American kestrels are gaining popularity and recognition as legitimate birds for falconry. As understanding of their ability and management increases, so will their use in the modern sport. The species' large wild populations and ease of captive breeding support this trend. Someday soon the notion of a hunting kestrel will be no more surprising than that of a hunting red-tailed hawk. Falconers will simply expect to catch starlings and sparrows with their kestrels, and if they fail, will look to themselves for the reason.

From that point, some will push on to the horizon. There is room to explore here. A true generalist, the American kestrel borrows at will from all other raptors whatever is necessary to make the catch. Already falconers are training kestrels to wait-on; some using kites to raise pitch. How long can it be before balloons or dogs are added to the formula? The kestrel's ability in a cast of two makes me wonder if three might not be the magic number for pursuit flights at quail? Imagine a group of sibling kestrels perched shoulder-to-shoulder, leaning toward the dog and a scaled quail just waiting to break. One lifetime is too short to try it all.

Whatever quarry future falconers pursue with their kestrels, starlings and house sparrows will figure prominently. In a way, we're fortunate to have them. Wilderness and rural areas will continue to recede beneath the tide of urban sprawl; native species may suffer, but these two foreigners will thrive. Falconers who see this tide rising around them have a choice: adapt to the new landscape, seek out what good it holds or find some lesser pastime to pursue.

Referenced Works

Bent, A.C. 1938. LIFE HISTORIES OF NORTH AMERICAN BIRDS OF PREY, PART TWO. Dover Publications Inc. New York, New York.

Balgooyen, T.G. 1976. BEHAVIOR AND ECOLOGY OF AMERICAN KESTREL. Univ. Calif. Publ. Zool. 103: 1-83

Bradshaw, B., 2001. ATHENA AND THE KITE. Hawk Chalk, 40(2): 63-64..

Coulson, J. 1996. Hawking Respectable Quarry with the American Kestrel. Ch.14:271-289 in DESERT HAWKING: WITH A LITTLE HELP FROM MY FRIENDS. Harry McElroy, publisher.

Dunning, J.B. (Ed). 1993. CRC HANDBOOK OF AVIAN BODY MASSES. CRC Press, Inc. Boca Raton, Florida.

Ford, E. 1992. FALCONRY ART AND PRACTICE. The Bath Press. London, England.

Henny, C.J., and H.M. Wight. 1972. Population Ecology and Environmental Pollution, Red-tailed Hawks and Cooper's Hawks. pp.229-250 in POPULATION ECOLOGY OF MIGRATORY BIRDS: A SYMPOSIUM. U. S. Dept. Interior, Fish and Wildlife Service.

Hoffman, M.L., and M.W. Collopy. 1987. Distribution and Nesting Ecology of the American Kestrel *(Falco sparverius paulus)* near Archer, Florida. pp.47-57 in Bird, D.M. and R.Bowman (eds.) THE ANCESTRAL KESTREL. Raptor Research Foundation and MacDonald Raptor Research Centre, Ste. Anne de Bellevue, Quebec.

Holler, Nicholas R. and Edward W. Schafer, Jr. 1982. POTENTIAL SECONDARY HAZARDS OF AVITROL BAITS TO SHARP-SHINNED HAWKS AND AMERICAN KESTRELS. J.Wildl. Manage. 46(2):457-462.WR 186.

James, F. C. 1970. GEOGRAPHIC SIZE VARIATION IN BIRDS AND ITS RELATION TO CLIMATE. Ecology 51:365-390.

Johnsgard, Paul A. 1990. HAWKS, EAGLES AND FALCONS OF NORTH AMERICA. pp 276-284. Smithsonian Institution. Washington, D.C.

Mullenix, M. 1997. HAWKING WITH THE COMMON KESTREL *(Falco tinnunculus)*. Hawk Chalk 36(3):44-47.

Mullenix, M., and B.A. Millsap. 1995. RELATIVE DISPOSITION OF AMERICAN KESTRELS AND RED-TAILED HAWKS UNDER FALCONRY MANAGEMENT. Florida Game and Fresh Water Fish Commission. Tallahassee, Florida.

Redig, P.T. 1994. DISEASES AND AILMENTS OF RAPTORS. Ch.35:321-334 in NORTH AMERICAN FALCONRY AND HUNTING HAWKS. North American Falconry and Hunting Hawks, publisher. Denver, CO.

Smallwood, J.A. 1987. SEXUAL SEGREGATION BY AMERICAN KESTRELS *(Falco sparverius)* Wintering in South Central Florida: Vegetative Structure and Responses to Differential Prey Availability. Condor 89:842-849.

Smith, D.G., and J.R. Murphy. 1973. BREEDING ECOLOGY OF RAPTORS IN UTAH. Brigham Young Univ. Sci. Bull. Biol. Set. 18(3).

Stys, B. 1993. ECOLOGY AND HABITAT PROTECTION NEEDS OF THE SOUTHEASTERN AMERICAN KESTREL (*Falco sparverius paulus*) ON LARGE-SCALE DEVELOPMENT SITES IN FLORIDA. Florida Game and Fresh Water Fish Commission, Nongame Wildlife Program Technical Report No. 13. 35 pp. Tallahassee, Florida.

Tuttle, K. 1996. CLASSICAL PHEASANT HAWKING WITH PASSAGE PRAIRIE FALCONS. Ch.120:367-389 in DESERT HAWKING: WITH A LITTLE HELP FROM MY FRIENDS. Harry McElroy, publisher.

Village, A. 1990. THE KESTREL. T & AD Poyser Ltd. London, England.

Appendix 1: The Kestrels

The information included in this book was obtained by observing the training and hunting of over 20 American kestrels, 8 of which were flown by myself. The following table briefly outlines my trained kestrels' careers.

Source & Sex	Quarry Taken Taken	Duration Flown (months)	Initial Weight (grams)	Hunting Weight	Disposition
Captive Bred Male "Beaumont"	17 house sparrows	4	116	85	Returned to breeder
Captive Bred Female "Sally"	390 various birds	25	126	95	Lost in summer soar
Passage Female "Fox"	17 various birds	2	117	97	Lost with starling in billboard
Haggard Female "Mrs. Robinson"	99 various birds	3.5	165	125	Lost with sparrow on rooftop
Passage Male "Tycho"	280 various birds	14	111	86	Killed by trained female
Passage Female "Ella"	89 various birds	3.5	145	104	Released
Passage Female "Nova"	77 various birds	2.5	141	103	Released
Haggard Female "Phoebe"	671 various birds	20	100	85	Released

Appendix 2: A Kestrel's First Month

The following notes document one month of the training, entering and hunting of a passage female American kestrel. This kestrel was flown at quarry sooner than others I've had, though tight weight control and good slips generally substituted for a more reliable scheme of manning and repetition. Such shortcuts may reduce training time, but probably increase the initial risk of loss.

20 December
9:30 am (141 grams)
Caught and released four adults before trapping this juvenile off a lightpole at the airport; this is the same kestrel that gives Brian's merlin hell everyday that we fly her nearby. She hit the trap almost as soon as it hit the ground; I jessed, hooded, boxed and took her home. She took a few tidbits after an hour of learning how to stand comfortably on the glove. Takes the hood well so far. She is in good feather, hog-fat and barrel-chested. Last kestrel trapped at this weight ("Ella" @ 145g) flew at 104 grams.

21 December
7:30 am (132g)
Hopped back up to the perch last night a few times, but still bates hard away at the slightest disturbance. Ate readily off the fist this morning.

22 December
7:30 am (129g)
Readily grabbed food off the glove last night. Took tidbits from my fingers and then hopped the full length of the leash four or five times, but response slowed quickly thereafter. Hopped back up to the perch several times after bating, but spent most of the evening biting at her jesses on the ground. This morning: still bating and crouching defensively. Falls asleep quickly when hooded.

1:00 pm (125g)
Flew length of leash 3 times, hesitantly.

23 December
7:00 am (125g)
2:45 pm (123g)
Hopping full length of leash with total attention.

24 December
7:00 am (121g)
Much bating in the morning. Still crouches when approached.
3:45 pm (121g)
Flew full length of room 3-4 times without hesitation.
11:00 pm (120.5g)

25 December
7:30 am (118.5g)
1:45 pm (116g)
Good response across room. Fed to 120g.
10:43 pm (118g)

26 December
7:30 am (115.5g)
10:30 am (115g)
Flew 4 times across room with immediate response. Fed to 117g.
2:10 pm (115.5g)
5:10 pm (115g)
Good response to lure and across-room flights. Fed to 118g.

27 December
8:00 am (114.5g)
12:45 pm (112.5g)
Flew to the fist and lure with Shelly in the room; fed to 118g.

28 December
12:00n

Noticed leg scale damage where top of jesses has abraded skin. Swelling, scale separation and redness found on both legs. I changed jesses and applied antibiotic cream regularly. As I had checked for damage at every opportunity over the last week, I presume the abrasions are new.

6:00 pm (112.5g)

Flew to the fist immediately inside; was aggressive on the lure. Fed to 116g.

29 December
7:30 am (111.5g)

Flew about 10 feet to the fist and lure outside on the creance. Response was not immediate, but not too bad considering it was her first time flying outside. The kestrel is pretty tame now, "puffed out" even when outdoors, and looking for tidbits when whistled at. Leg scale damage appears somewhat better. Swelling is gone, and she does not favor one leg over the other. Fed to 115g.

5:00 pm (109g)

Flew full length of creance several times to the fist and lure. Flew free without mishap, but kestrel was nervous immediately afterward; probably still too high.

30 December
4:00pm (107g)

Flew from the car toward a flock of sparrows, then checked on a mole cricket and ate it. Returned immediately to car when called. First free flight under field conditions; first time returning to vehicle.

31 December
4:00pm (105g)
I winged a starling and sent the kestrel after it on the ground. She saw the bird, slicked down her feathers and bobbed her head, but would not leave without a little push. Once on the wing she flew quickly at the bird, bound to it and began to eat. She did not try to carry as I approached. Fed her the head, heart and lungs to 112g.

1 January
5:00pm (105g)
1st kill. Flew off the fist at a starling trapped up in the rafters. She bound to it and hung there fighting it while I climbed up to retrieve her. Making-in under those conditions was not ideal, but it was unavoidable. Once on the ground I set her down and walked around her in circles, tid-bitting occasionally. She fed comfortably to approximately 112g.

2-5 January
(103–106g)
Kestrel took many good slips and pulled feathers from five birds, but held on to none. She understands the program now and is actively looking for ground-feeding birds. She takes slips without hesitation and seems to fly aggressively. Good return response.

6 January
9:30am (104g)
2nd kill. Took starling on the ground very well on second flight; really knows how to handle them. No trouble making-in. Fed to 112g.

7 January
9:00am (104g)
3rd kill. Took starling on first flight. Fed to 111g.
2:30pm (105g)
4th kill. Took another on the first flight. Controls birds very well. She was a bit spooky while I made in, but seems to be improving. Fed to 116g.

8 January
7:30am (106g)
Weight dropped quickly throughout the day; fed several tidbits to maintain 104-106 range.
4:00pm (104g)
5th kill. Took bird off tombstone in first flight. Fed to 124g.

9 January
8:00am (110g)
4:00pm
Took one flight at a flock of bathing starlings but would not commit.

10 January
5:00pm (104g)
6th kill. Took bird near the ground but on the rise; handled very well and did not carry when approached.

11 January
Afternoon (104g)
Took only two slips; missed on both.

12 January
Morning (105g)
7th kill. Took a starling on the ground on the way to the GFA meet.

13 January
Throughout the day (104–107g)
8th, 9th, 10th and 11th kills. Took birds well, catching all on the ground but with good speed; one bird was knocked about three feet into a bush with an audible hit. Went out with Jim in mid-morning and had trouble finding good slips; finally found a starling in the open and she plowed it under. Jim stayed for two more kills in the afternoon before heading back. Though I was supposedly done, I slipped her again on the way back to Steve's for a final kill. She stayed calm and well mannered while I fed her the remainder of the day's ration on the ground.

14 January
9:00 am & 4:30 pm (105g)
12th and 13th kills. One bird caught in the morning and another in the evening.

15 January
4:00 pm (105g)
Missed on several good slips; fed up on the way home. Had a chance to let her fly over a large turf farm area. She ranged about 200 yards, hovered, kited around and was chased briefly by a wild kestrel. She flew strong in the wind and returned from a distance as soon as the lure was presented. This was her longest flight in terms of distance and time aloft since being trapped. Though car hawking does not seem to build much muscle, her wing-strength appears good. Did over 60 jump-ups in the evening before wearing out.

16 January
2:00 pm (107g)
Did not fly at quarry. Tried jump-ups; did another 65 flights before her breathing seemed labored. She could have done more, but was fed too much by then at 120g.

17 January
7:30am (110g)
5:30pm (106g)
14th kill. Took bird on the ground after several misses on easy slips. Stayed uptight and bated all day from overfeeding. Fed to 112g that evening.

18 January
10:00am (105g)
15th kill. Took bird on the ground on the first slip.
2:00pm (106g)
Did 65 jump-ups until kestrel obviously fatigued. Fed to 112.5g

19 January
9:45am (105g)
16th kill. Took a great flight at a bird on the wing, chasing it under a car and around two bushes before pulling off. Missed some starlings on easy slips. Finally took a flight at a bird on a bush, chasing it down into the foliage and catching it as it tried to escape through a fence. I had to kill the bird, remove the kestrel's talons and call her through the fence to retrieve her. One deck feather bent at the tip while struggling with quarry through fence. Fed to 110g.

20 January
9:30am to 5:30 pm (102g–115g)
17th, 18th, 19th, 20th and 21st kills. This was basically a red-letter day all around. We flew her only while traveling from field to field to fly the other hawk on rabbits, but she flew hard and responded well every time. All birds were taken on the ground. She carried the first kill about three feet to hide behind a trash barrel, but then settled down and allowed me to approach while she fed. All others were taken with no trouble making-in. Fed her some of each kill, and tidbits to 122g that evening.

Appendix 3: Dispositions

Listed here are disposition records of falconry-harvested American kestrels and red-tailed hawks* from New Mexico (1971–1980), California (1978 & 1980) and Idaho (1980–1985). Individuals maintained in captivity are included in the totals, but not presented in the table.

American Kestrels

State	Lost/Released	Died	Total
New Mexico	9	3	14
California	90	10	174
Idaho	5	2	7
Totals	104 (53.3%)	15 (7.7%)	195

Red-tailed Hawks

State	Lost/Released	Died	Total
New Mexico	18	6	30
California	308	28	762
Idaho	15	1	30
Totals	341 (41.5%)	35 (4.3%)	822

*From Millsap, B. A. and M. Mullenix. 1995. Relative Dispositions of American Kestrels and Red-tailed Hawks Under Falconry Management. Florida Game and Fresh Water Fish Commission Report.

Appendix 4: Notes on Weight Control & Behavior

Individual Weight/Response Chart for Pheobe
South Eastern Female American Kestrel

RESPONSE TO FOOD[1]	CONDITION	DAILY FLYING WEIGHT[2] DAILY FOOD REQUIRED[3]
Able to maintain weight on tiny amounts of food	Non-responsive	90g
Gains weight even on small amounts of food	Too high - responds slowly	87-89g **7 - 10 g/d**
Maintains on set amount of food daily	Best response range	83-86g **12 - 14 g/d**
Requires increasingly more food	Too low - desparate, weak possibly aggressive	80-82g **15 - 16 g/d**
May not have enough energy to digest necessary amount of food	Starvation!	79g

[1]All food is freshly killed small birds
[2]The bird's weight at hunting time each day.
[3]**Number of grams fed per day to maintain this weight.**

Appendix 5: Hood Patterns

Beak Opening #1
4.6 Small Female or Male

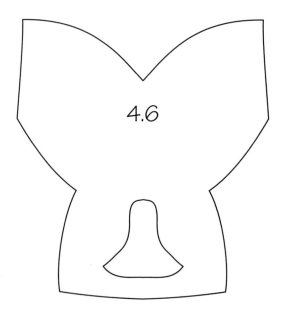

4.6

Appendix 5: Hood Patterns

Beak Opening #1
4.8 Average Either Sex

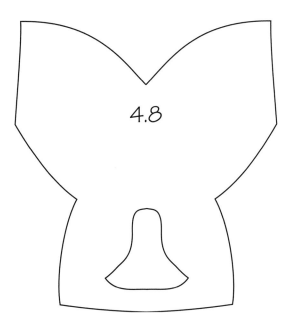

4.8

Appendix 5: Hood Patterns

Beak Opening #1
5.0 Large Female

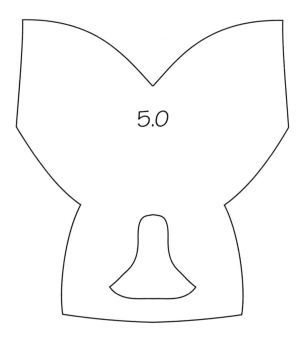

5.0

Appendix 5: Hood Patterns

Beak Opening #2
4.6 Small Female or Male

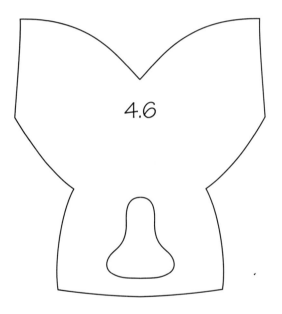

4.6

Appendix 5: Hood Patterns

Beak Opening #2
4.8 Average Either Sex

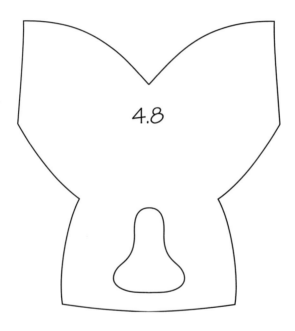

4.8

Appendix 5: Hood Patterns

Beak Opening #2
5.0 Large Female

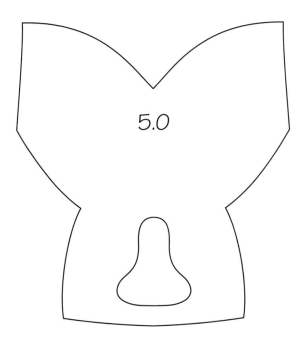

5.0